Battleground Europe

Walking Arras

A GUIDE TO THE 1917 ARRAS BATTLEFIELDS

Battleground series:

Battleground Europe

Walking Arras

A GUIDE TO THE 1917 ARRAS BATTLEFIELDS

PAUL REED

Series Editor
Nigel Cave

Pen & Sword
MILITARY

For Kieron with my love

Other titles in the battleground series by Paul Reed:
Walking the Somme
Walking the Salient
Somme - Courcelette
Somme - Combles

First published in Great Britain in 2007 and reprinted in 2013 by
PEN & SWORD MILITARY
An imprint of
Pen & Sword Books Ltd
47 Church Street, Barnsley
South Yorkshire
S70 2AS

ISBN 978 1 84415 619 1

A CIP catalogue record for this book is
available from the British Library

Typeset in Times

Printed and bound in England
By CPI Group (UK) Ltd, Croydon, CR0 4YY

Pen & Sword Books Ltd incorporates the Imprints of Pen & Sword Aviation,
Pen & Sword Family History, Pen & Sword Maritime, Pen & Sword Military,
Pen & Sword Discovery, Pen & Sword Politics, Pen & Sword Archaeology,
Pen & Sword Atlas, Wharncliffe Local History, Wharncliffe True Crime,
Wharncliffe Transport, Pen & Sword Select, Pen & Sword Military Classics,
Leo Cooper, The Praetorian Press, Claymore Press, Remember When,
Seaforth Publishing and Frontline Publishing

For a complete list of Pen & Sword titles please contact
PEN & SWORD BOOKS LIMITED
47 Church Street, Barnsley, South Yorkshire, S70 2AS, England
E-mail: enquiries@pen-and-sword.co.uk
Website: www.pen-and-sword.co.uk

CONTENTS

Ruins of Hotel de Ville in Arras town square.

INTRODUCTION BY SERIES EDITOR

Of all the major great battles fought by the BEF in the Great War, that of Arras, in the spring of 1917, is the most neglected. It still awaits a full scale academic work (though John Nicholls' excellent *Cheerful Sacrifice* does provide a good overview); perhaps it shall not be too long in coming, as scholarly interest in the First World War continues to flourish and grow.

What popular knowledge there is of the Battle of Arras has tended to be dominated by the success of the Canadian Corps (greatly enlarged for the occasion by a mass of British troops, particularly artillery but also huge numbers supporting the logistics) at Vimy. Without a doubt, of course, this was a triumph for Byng and the Canadian infantry under his command – only one British brigade took part in the assault – and of his artillery commanders.

Arras was a battle in which the daily casualty rates (4,076) were considerably higher than those of the Somme (2,963), Third Ypres (2,323) and the Hundred Days of the Advance to Victory (3,645) in the summer and autumn of 1918. It had begun well and had certainly induced a state of near panic amongst the higher German command at the end of the first day; but then that remarkable organisation, the German Imperial Army, got a grip and the campaign fell into the pattern of the seemingly traditional attritional grind. Now is not the time to go into the whys and the wherefores of the battle, its role in Nivellei flawed grand scheme and the disastrous consequences of the lead up to the battle for relations between senior army commanders and the politicians (notably Lloyd George). Arras was a battle which illustrated the improving techniques of the BEF and its composite parts, showed the need to understand the possibilities and limitations of the tank better, illustrated flaws in command systems and did no good at all for the relationship of Gough with the Australians and – at first – the military career of Third Army's commander, Allenby.

This book does not concern itself overly with these matters. Paul Reed once more takes us over paths trodden by men who were asked to make a huge – and, for all too many, the ultimate – sacrifice. He brings to bear his formidable talents as a battlefield guide and will certainly have done his 'bit' in ensuring that the men of the Battle of Arras are not forgotten by future generations.

Nigel Cave,
Trivandrum

6

INTRODUCTION

The Battle of Arras falls between the Somme and Third Ypres; it marked the first British attempt to storm the Hindenburg Line defences, and the first use of lessons learned from the events of 1916. But it remains a forgotten part of the Western Front, with far fewer visitors compared to Ypres and the Somme. It also remains one of the great killing battles of the Great War, with such a high fatal casualty rate that a soldier's chances of surviving Arras were much slimmer than even the Somme or Passchendaele. Yet few have heard of it, little is published on the battle and the cemetery visitors' books indicate only a trickle of pilgrims.

For a battlefield that, even outside the events of April-May 1917 (which principally concern this volume), was one of the most important British sectors of the Old Front Line, this is somewhat strange. Most soldiers who served in the Great War served at Arras at some point; either on their way to or from the Somme in 1916, in the fighting of Spring 1917, or when war returned for the Kaiser's Battle in March 1918 and the Allied Offensive of that summer. It was a name very much in the consciousness of the survivors of the Great War, and a centre for many old comrades who returned in the 1920s and 30s.

Ninety years later, while there has been development at Arras, it is still an impressive battlefield and one worthy of the attention of any Great War enthusiast. With ground the texture of the Somme – rolling chalk downland, with huge open fields and a few woods – it is also good for walking and, finally, this book will give a lead in seeing the ground connected with the fighting in 1917. It marks a slight departure from the style of my previous two walking books, in that the chapters look at the historical background of an area and then separately describe a walk; with supplementary notes about the associated cemeteries in that region. This, I hope, makes the book more accessible to those who want to use it as a guidebook to Arras and do not want to have to walk the ground. But walking remains the best way to see any battlefield, and I hope this might inspire you to see some of the Arras area on foot.

Walking Arras marks the final volume in a trilogy of walking books about the British sector of the Western Front. Our journey has taken us from the flat plains of Flanders, along the mud-soaked lanes of the Somme, to the open fields of Artois here at Arras. For now it is time to hang up the walking boots, and to look to fields fresh with the rumours of other wars. But the 'Old Battalion' will march again; on ground beyond the Great War, but always in its shadow in some strange way or other. I hope to see you there; on the beaches or in the bocage.

For now it is journey's end; and as the sun sets across the beautiful memorial which crowns the crest of Vimy Ridge, I think back across more than two decades of wandering the front and speaking to veterans. The time has come when almost the last of them has faded away; but we still owe them a debt, a duty. The torch is passing, and now it is us who most mourn over the soldiers' cemeteries of France and Flanders and echo Henry Williamson's words:

'Oh my comrades! My comrades in Ancient Sunlight...'

Paul Reed
Kent, The Somme & Artois
Summer 2004

Old Front Line website
http://battlefields1418.50megs.com

'Barbed Wire Square' – the main square at Arras where soldiers congregated on the eve of the battle.

Troops arriving for the battle in March 1917.

Acknowledgements

As always, a book of this type takes many years to complete and I am grateful to a number of friends who have assisted. Of those who have walked and visited the battlefields at Arras with me I would like to mention: Geoff Bridger, the late Stephen Clarke, Brian Fullagher, Clive Harris, members of the Henry Williamson Society, Tony and Joan Poucher, the late Terry Russell, Frank & Lou Stockdale, Terry Whippy and Andrew Whittington.

In France thanks goes to: Andre Coilliott of Beaurains, Bernard Delsert of Cambrai, Tom and Janet Fairgrieve at Delville Wood, Jean Letaille at Bullecourt and Jean-Pierre Matte at Bernafay Wood. In Germany my good friend and colleague Alexander Fasse has also helped with German sources, for which I am particularly grateful.

I was privileged to interview a number of Arras veterans, sadly all of whom have 'faded away' like all old soldiers. As the years progress, and I study the war more and more, I realise how lucky I was to have known them and how much they enriched my knowledge of the war. In particular I would like to mention: W.A.Baker (Royal Scots); George Butler (12th MGC); Harry Coates (London Scottish); Horace Hamm (12th Middlesex); Frank Plumb (11th Suffolks); and Macolm Vyvyan MC (96th SB RGA).

Finally my love and thanks goes to Kieron, soon to be an author in her own right, and to Ed and Poppy who follow us around the battlefields. Poppy in particular has spent much of her young life walking Arras with me, and I hope it has made a lasting impression!

USERS GUIDE

GETTING THERE: Arras is perhaps one of the easiest battlefields to reach from the traditional start point for British visitors, Calais. From the Euro Tunnel terminal or ferry port it is around 110km and can be reached in just over an hour on the A26 motorway. Alternatively, you could extend your journey and make your way via the Route Nationales. Going via Étaples, one could see the site of the Bull Ring and the huge Lutyens designed cemetery before making your way to Montreuil. Then follow the N39 via Hesdin and St Pol (where there are also interesting military cemeteries) for the final part of the journey to Arras itself. This could easily occupy the first day of your visit, and is recommended.

ACCOMMODATION: While some visitors might choose to do some of the walks in this book from their favourite base on the Somme, Arras is a delightful place to stay with a variety of accommodation possibilities. A full list can be obtained from the tourist office (see below). There are no British run B&Bs in the area (yet!), but there are a couple of French run Gite de France Chambre d'hôtes in the outlying villages, including:
Bed & Breakfast – Bullecourt
Mr & Mme Therlier
'La Nicolinere', 52 Route de Douai, 62128 Bullecourt, France.
Tel: 0033 3 21 48 91 27

EATING OUT: Arras abounds with restaurants and a full list is available from the tourist office. Traditional French food dominates, but Arras has several Chinese, Italian and Vietnamese restaurants near the railway station or in the main squares. For those on a budget, 'frites' (chip) wagons are found on many of the main streets! Bars are also numerous, with an Irish one close to the railway square.

GETTING ABOUT: Arras boasts quite a good public transport system, with several of the villages in the northern battlefield area having their own railway stations (but trains are infrequent). There is also a bus service, with the main stops close to the station. Several of the villages featured in the book are served by these buses. Cars can be hired from offices near the station, and for bikes ask at the tourist office.

TOURIST OFFICE: There is an excellent tourist office at Arras located on the ground floor of the Hotel de Ville (town hall). Here English is spoken, there are English leaflets and some of the publications mentioned in the Reading List can be purchased along with the CWGC Cemetery Map Book covering Belgium and France. The office is normally closed for lunch, except during the summer months. For information contact:

Office de Tourisme d'Arras
Hotel de Ville
Place des Heros
62000 Arras
Tel: (0033) 3 21 51 26 95.
Fax: (0033) 3 21 51 76 49.
Web: www.ot-arras.fr

COMMONWEALTH WAR GRAVES COMMISSION: The CWGC main French office is in the suburbs of Arras at Beaurains. Here you can trace a war grave, purchase the CWGC Cemetery Map Book, cemetery registers and request free leaflets. Opening hours vary, and it is normally closed on French public holidays. Ring before you visit. The address is:

Commonwealth War Graves Commission
Rue Angele Richard
62217 Beaurains
France
Tel: (03) 21 21 77 00
Fax: (03) 21 21 77 10
E-mail: faoffice@cwgc.org
Web: www.cwgc.org

THE IRON HARVEST: While a bomb disposal unit still operates in this part of France, because it is a infrequently visited battlefield the fields are littered with far more material than on the Somme. Live shells, grenades, mortar bombs and other munitions are quite common, and should be left alone. A farmer was nearly killed at Monchy-le-Preux in 1998 when his plough detonated a British 18-pounder shell. These items were designed to kill, and this should always be remembered.

The Iron Harvest on The Pimple – a French grenade from the 1915 battles.

THE WALKS: The Arras battlefield is similar to the Somme, but has seen a great deal of development in the past fifteen years. Much of the area has been swallowed up by new housing, the motorway and the more recent fast rail link to Paris. Industrial areas now dominate Orange Hill, and a second development has begun to the south close to Wancourt. However, there are still many quiet parts of the old front line to explore, with numerous fascinating cemeteries and memorials.

THE WESTERN FRONT ASSOCIATION: For those with more than a passing interest in the Great War, membership of the Western Front Association is essential. Founded by author John Giles in 1980, the WFA has branches all over the United Kingdom, and indeed overseas – some of which meet on a monthly basis. The annual subscription includes copies of the in-house newsletter, The Bulletin, and the glossy magazine, Stand To! Members also have access to the WFA's collection of trench maps and cheap photocopies of them are available – including many of the Arras battlefield. For further details contact:

The Western Front Association, Membership Administration
6 Church Street, Kidderminster DY10 2AD United Kingdom
Web: www.westernfrontassociation.com

A pictorial map of the Arras battlefield.

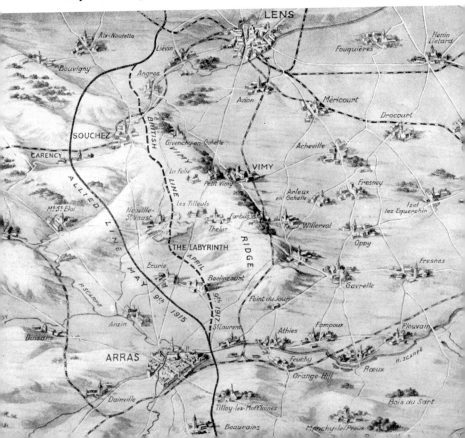

Chapter 1

CANADIAN CORPS: VIMY RIDGE
9TH/14TH APRIL 1917

The Battle

Any study of a battlefield soon highlights that high ground is all important; whichever side commands that high ground, often dominates the battlefield from a military point of view. At Arras there were two areas of such high ground; the Notre Dame de Lorette spur to the north, and Vimy Ridge to the north-east. The German I and VI Army Corps captured this area in September 1914, facing the X and XXI French Army Corps during the so-called 'Race to the Sea'. The Germans then sat in occupation of these two ridges, and the French spent much of 1915 trying to reclaim them. First there was an attack on Notre Dame de Lorette on 9th May 1915, just as the British Army was assaulting the Aubers Ridge further to the north. The French X Army Corps, spear-headed by General Barbot's 77th Division, attacked the Lorette spur, taking much of the ground, but at high cost – Barbot himself was killed at the head of his troops in Souchez. Meanwhile the 39th Division had taken Neuville St Vaast and on their left flank the Moroccan Division had fought their way onto the lower slopes of Hill 145 - the highest point on Vimy Ridge. Successive German counter-attacks threw the French back, and while Notre Dame de Lorette remained in their hands, Vimy eluded them in this operation. A further

Mine crater on The Pimple – evidence of the fighting here in 1915/16.

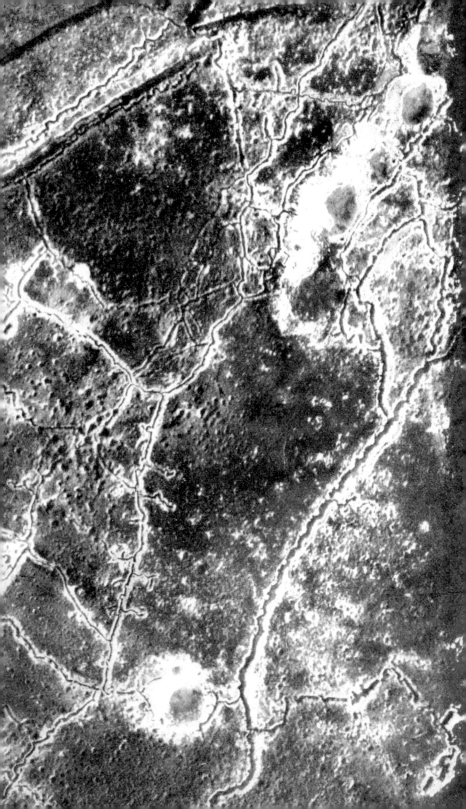

attack on 25th September also failed, fought as a joint operation with the British at Loos. By the close of the year the French had lost nearly a quarter of a million men in Artois in 1915, with the Germans still dominating the Arras battlefield from Vimy Ridge.

In the early months of 1916 British troops began to take over the sector around Arras, as the line was extended south from Loos. The Vimy Ridge area was now divided into a number of sectors. To the north was The Pimple, in the centre was the ground below Hill 145, then the trenches opposite La Folie Farm, with the lines extending down to the Arras-Lens road close to Thelus. The 46th (North Midland) Division took over the area at Vimy Ridge from the positions at Hill 145 to La Folie Farm, with the 47th (London) Division occupying the line to the north at The Pimple. Other British divisions were then rotated through these sectors, and men from the Tunnelling Companies of the Royal Engineers came down to the ridge and found the ground here particularly suitable for their type of warfare. Mines were blown by both sides on almost a daily basis in early 1916, as evidence on the crest of Vimy Ridge shows to this day. A typical experience of this is described by the London Division in April 1916.

The first German mine went up on April 26th. The 140th Brigade were about to relieve the 141st Brigade at the time, but the danger had been anticipated, and a supporting company of the 6th Battalion [London Regiment] was sent up in advance. Our front line was broken by the explosion, but the crater was

After the capture of the mine craters in May 1916, German troops fortified them.

immediately seized, and the near lip consolidated. Rifle-fire from
the 17th and 19th Battalions protected the consolidation, and
prevented any counter-attack. The crater was called New Cut
Crater. On the 29th our miners blew a camouflet some hundred
yards north of this, which detonated a Boche mine, and formed
Broadridge Crater. By way of retaliation the enemy sprang a
third mine between the two. This destroyed part of the front line,
and the 6th Battalion suffered over eighty casualties.[1]

However, on the whole this was considered a 'quiet' sector. There were
daily bombardments, patrol work, mines going off, exchanges of fire
from both sides and trench raids, but no major operations. The only
event of note prior to the fighting in 1917 was the German attack on
positions along the northern sector of Vimy Ridge in May 1916. On
21st May German units attacked the positions below Hill 145 between
Broadmarsh and Momber Craters and against the positions of the 47th
(London) Division at The Pimple.

At 3.40pm the bombardment became intense... They came
over in great force, and the weight of the attack fell upon the 7th
and 8th Battalions, who had lain for four hours in unprotected
trenches, under a bombardment far heavier than any we had ever
known before. These battalions, together with the troops on their
right [from the 25th Division] *were driven out of the front line*
trench, across two supports, into a line half-way down the slope.[2]

Counter-attacks began that evening, and further battalions came up to
assist in the early hours of 22nd May. Casualties amongst the 8th
Battalion London Regiment (Post Office Rifles) were particularly
heavy, their battalion commander being among the wounded. While
further counter-attacks regained some ground, the Division was finally
relieved on 25th May by 2nd Division. By this time it had suffered
more than 2,100 casualties in the fighting at Vimy Ridge.

But the Battle of the Somme was now looming close, and mine
warfare on the ridge gradually reduced as men and resources were sent
south. British troops continued to occupy the trenches, with the 60th
(London) Division now holding the main sector at Vimy. One of the
last British units to serve in the Vimy sector before the Canadians
arrived were the 2nd Leinsters of the 24th Division. Captain Francis
Hitchcock of this battalion describes life here in late September 1916.

My company front lay in a very interesting sector. The
trenches were very dry, and well built, and on the right of my
front were five large mine craters, called from left to right,
'Gunner', 'Love', 'Momber', 'The Twins'. We held the near lips

16

of these craters by T head saps... running out from the front line. There was sufficient accommodation for the men in numbers of small, but deep, dug-outs, and a few disused mine shafts... A regiment of the Saxon Corps was opposite to us. They seemed very tame... It was all very weird; here we were on the lip of a large mine crater, the enemy holding the opposite lip, with... a few yards of air between their rifles' muzzles and our own.[3]

In October 1916 soldiers from the Canadian Corps, commanded by Lieutenant General Sir Julian Byng, began to arrive in the Vimy Ridge sector, fresh from their experiences at Courcelette and Regina Trench on the Somme; a battle which had cost the Canadians more than 24,000 casualties. The 4th (Canadian) Division was the last to arrive in late November, and preparations were made to hold the line here during the forthcoming winter, which would prove the coldest of the war.

At the same time plans were being made for an offensive in the Arras area, to take place in the early months of 1917. A conference at First Army headquarters had drawn up a plan for a two Corps attack, with Byng's Canadians being assigned the task of taking Vimy Ridge. Before him lay a formidable objective, which had so far eluded all earlier attacks.

German stretcher party evacuates wounded from Vimy Ridge, May 1916.

The Canadians take over – CEF soldiers newly arrived on the Vimy front late 1916.

Along the whole German front line it would have been difficult to find terrain better suited to defence, combining the advantages of observation and concealment. The crest of the ridge was formed by two heights, Hill 135, immediately north of the village of Thélus, and Hill 145, two miles farther north-west. The western slopes facing the Allied lines rose gradually over open ground which afforded excellent fields of fire for small arms and artillery. The reverse slope dropped sharply into the Douai plain, its thick woods providing adequate cover for the enemy's guns... At its other extremity the Ridge extended beyond Hill 145 to The Pimple, west of Givenchy, whence the ground fell quickly to the valley of the Souchez.[4]

On a front of more than 7,000 yards, Byng's four Canadian divisions would advance on their objectives. The centre position lay opposite Vimy village, on the east side of the ridge, with the north at The Pimple opposite Givenchy-en-Gohelle, and to the south opposite Thélus and Farbus. Further east was the German second line, anchored around the *Zwischen-Stellung* between Vimy and Thélus, and the Vimy-Riegel protecting Lens. Byng planned to attack these positions in four stages, dictated by the German zones of defence and their timing affected by the progress of XVII Corps on the left flank (see chapter 2). The Black Line, the initial objective, was on average 750 yards from the existing Canadian front line and covered the forward defence zone established by the Germans. The second objective, the Red Line, ran north along the *Zwischen-Stellung* and went north-east to take in La Folie Farm and Hill 145. For the left flank attack of the Canadian Corps (3rd and 4th Divisions) this would mark the final

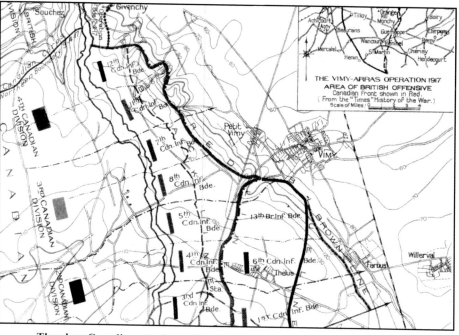

The plan: Canadian attack on Vimy Ridge 9th April 1917.

objective, but on the right were two more: the Blue Line and the Brown Line. The Blue Line included Thélus, Hill 135 and the wooded area of Bois du Goulot, and the Brown followed the German second line at Farbus Wood, Bois de la Ville and the southern part of Bois de Bonval.

Timings would be crucial, and Byng's staff had set up a strict time-table for the operation, with zero hour at 5.30am. The Black Line must be taken in the first 35 minutes, followed by a 40 minute pause to allow the objective to be secured. The Red Line would then be reached 20 minutes later; thus, following further consolidation, it was planned that by 7.05am the 3rd and 4th Divisions would be in control of the northern part of the Ridge. Meanwhile 1st and 2nd Divisions on the right would continue, following a two and a half hour pause on the Red Line to allow reserves to come up, and leap forward 1,200 yards to the Blue Line. After a further 96 minute pause, to allow the bombardment to continue and guns to get up, these same units would move in on the final objective on the Brown Line. If all went to plan Vimy Ridge would be in the Canadians' hands by 1.18pm, following an advance of more than 4,000 yards.

The key to success was the bombardment, just as it had been on the Somme in 1916. But the lesson which senior commanders like Byng had learnt from the Somme battle had been that an attack could only

19

German sentries in the front line on Vimy Ridge.

succeed if enough guns were assembled, and were of sufficient calibre; the British Army had lacked heavy guns the year before, which had seriously hampered operations in the early phase of the Somme. By early 1917 this was not as much of a problem, and for the assault on Vimy Byng not only had his divisional artillery, dedicated Canadian Siege Batteries (heavy guns), but also a large number of British Heavy Artillery Groups (HAGs) which consisted of guns from 6-inch to 15-inch. In total, Byng had 245 heavy guns and howitzers at his disposal, along with 480 18-pounders, and 138 4.5-inch howitzers. An additional 132 heavy guns and 102 field guns were provided by the British I Corps, and more heavy guns in reserve from the First Army pool. This gave a barrage density of one heavy gun per 20 yards of front, and one field gun per ten yards; an unparalleled concentration of artillery. Wire cutting would be performed by the new No 106 shrapnel fuse, and 'creeping barrages' or 'rolling barrages' were now commonplace and would be used to protect the infantry. More than a million shells would be fired into the German defences along the Ridge, creating what German accounts called 'the week of suffering'.

Byng also decided to utilise the system of tunnels that existed below the Canadian positions on the Ridge, just as other British commanders were doing in and around Arras itself. The Royal Engineer Tunnellers and Canadian Engineers worked tirelessly in the build-up to the attack, preparing a number of different systems so that the bulk of the Canadian Corps could approach the battlefield and be sheltered safe below ground on the eve of the operation. All the subways were lit, there were ammunition and supply depots, Regimental Aid Posts, headquarters, signals posts and miles of telephone line allowing clear and safe communications from the rear echelon towards the front line. One cave alone, the Zivy Cave near Neuville St Vaast, could house an entire battalion.

Canadian units had trained tirelessly for the attack, and the old fears about security had been put aside by Byng and his Staff, with all ranks from battalion commander down to private soldier briefed on the full details of the operation. The only piece of information withheld was the timing, which would only be given out at the last moment. This

Part of the tunnel and cave system used by the Canadians on the eve of the battle.

done, on the night of 8th April 1917 some 15,000 Canadian soldiers moved up in the tunnel systems and the trenches on the Ridge,

> ... *confident in the knowledge that everything possible had been done to assure success.*[5]

All units were in position by 4am, with the minimum of pre-attack casualties caused by speculative fire and machine-guns firing wild.

At 5.30am the men of Byng's Canadian Corps went over the top, into a snow blizzard on most parts of the Ridge, and for the first and only time in the Great War all four Canadian divisions fought side by side. Major General Arthur Currie's 1st Division did well in the early

Canada advance! Troops of the Canadian Corps assault Vimy Ridge, 9th April 1917.

stages of the advance, attacking a mile long front and closely following the barrage. There were six assaulting battalions, from left to right: 5th, 7th, 10th, 15th, 14th and 16th Battalions. It was found that the majority of the defenders were still sheltering in their dugouts when the front line trench was reached; many prisoners were taken and there was very little resistance. However, as the advance continued the amount of opposition increased with snipers and machine-guns firing at almost point-blank range. The experience of the 14th Battalion (Royal Montreal Regiment) is typical.

Driving through the German front line, No 3 Company brushed aside such opposition as the garrison afforded and advanced against a trench known as Eisener Kreuz Weg. Here

the defending Bavaraian troops fought gallantly, holding back the Canadian advance until killed or wounded by bomb or bayonet. In the hand to hand fighting the Royal Montrealers soon established superiority, but the enemy, by clever use of his machine-guns, forced payment for the ground torn from his grasp.[6]

One machine-gun in particular was causing heavy casualties to both the 14th and 15th Battalions until one officer of the Royal Montrealers rushed it.

Realising how serious an obstacle this gun presented, Lieut B.F. Davidson organised and led an attack against it. Game to the last, the gun crew met the Canadian assault with a shower of bombs, which dropped several of the Royal Montrealers in their tracks. Lieut Davidson, however, penetrated the grenade barrage, shot the crew, and put the gun out of action.[7]

Close by other brave deeds were being performed by men of the 16th Battalion (Canadian Scottish). The battalion was pinned down by fire in the area of Visener Graben, until Private W.J. Milne went forward. For his bravery in the ensuing action he was awarded the Victoria Cross. His citation reads,

For most conspicuous bravery and devotion to duty in attack. On approaching the first objective, Private Milne observed an enemy machine-gun firing on our advancing troops. Crawling on hands and knees, he succeeded in reaching the gun, killing the crew with bombs, and capturing the gun. On the line reforming, he again located a machine-gun in the support line, and stalking this second gun as he had done the first, he succeeded in putting the crew out of action and capturing the gun. His wonderful bravery and resource on these two occasions undoubtedly saved the lives of many of his comrades.[8]

Born in Scotland, Milne had emigrated to Canada in 1910 and worked as a farmer in Saskatchewan. He enlisted in September 1915, and joined the 16th Battalion at Ypres in the summer of 1916. He served at Courcelette and Regina Trench, and came north with his battalion to Vimy in late 1916. During the action for the second machine-gun, Milne fell dead. His body was never found and he is commemorated on the Vimy Memorial.

Pte W.J.Milne VC (NAC).

By 6.15am Currie's men had reached the Black Line. They resumed their advance half an hour later, and headed for the Intermediate Line protecting Thelus. Smoke and falling snow covered their attack, and the Bavarian troops defending the village did not see them coming until 1st Division was almost on top of them. By 7am the Red Line at the *Zwischen-Stellung* had fallen, and a whole German battalion was seen retreating in the direction of Farbus Wood. With high spirits, the first phase of operations on the right flank were completed.

The neighbouring 2nd Division, commanded by Major General Sir H.E. Burstall, had also done well. Their front was 1,400 yards wide with the 4th and 5th Brigades in the vanguard of the advance.

Walking, running and occasionally jumping across No Man's Land, the men followed closely the whitish-grey puffs that marked the exploding shrapnel of the barrage. Co-operating aeroplanes swooped low, sounding their klaxon horns and endeavouring to mark the progress of the troops in the driving snowstorm... Opposition stiffened at the second German line, and as on other sectors of the front, only timely acts of individual daring and initiative kept the advance going.[9]

One such act was on the 18th Battalion (Western Ontario) front. Lance Sergeant E.W. Sifton was a Canadian, born in Wallacetown, Ontario, in 1891. He enlisted in October 1914, and served on the Western Front from 1915. In the attack on Vimy Ridge, the 18th Battalion came under enfilade machine-gun fire, inflicting heavy losses. At this point Sifton stepped in and his bravery resulted in the award of a Victoria Cross. His citation reads,

For most conspicuous bravery and devotion to duty. During the attack on enemy trenches, Sgt Sifton's company was held up by machine-gun fire, which inflicted many casualties. Having located the gun, he charged it single-handed, killing all the crew. A small enemy party advanced down the trench, but he succeeded in keeping those off till our troops had gained the position. In carrying out this gallant act he was killed, but his conspicuous valour undoubtedly saved many lives and contributed largely to the success of the operation.[10]

L/Sgt E.W.Sifton VC (NAC).

Buried on the battlefield in a mass grave located in a former mine crater in No Man's Land, Sifton's name can be found on the wall at Lichfield Crater Cemetery.

The 2nd Division also reached the Black Line by 6.15am, and from here were to continue to the Red Line at *Turko-Graben* close to the village of Les Tilleuls. This next phase began 30 minutes later, and the

21st Battalion (Eastern Ontario) soon entered the village, to find a large cave which housed two German battalion headquarters, and resulted in some 106 prisoners being taken. Meanwhile, 25th Battalion (Nova Scotia) had taken Turko-Graben, along with two 77mm field guns and eight machine-guns. The 22nd Battalion (French Canadians) arrived to help mop-up, and some 400 prisoners were taken here. But in the 25th Battalion alone, casualties up to this point had amounted to more than 250 officers and men; which indicated the strength with which the defenders held their ground.

Further to the north, opposite La Folie Farm and Bois de la Folie, Major L.J. Lipsett's 3rd Division began their advance. 7th Brigade attacked on the left, with the Royal Canadian Regiment (RCR) and Princess Patricia's Canadian Light Infantry (PPCLI) in the first wave and 42nd (Royal Highlanders of Canada) to follow. On the right was 8th Brigade, made up entirely of battalions of the Canadian Mounted Rifles (CMR), with 1st, 2nd and 4th CMR going forward together. Emerging from their tunnel systems below the ridge and into the forward trenches, No Man's Land – a mass of mine craters - was soon crossed and the German positions entered. In some cases the bombardment had been so destructive that it proved difficult actually to recognise some of the objectives, but this was only a minor problem and the Black Line at *Zwischen-Stellung* was in Lipsett's hands by 6.25am.

Canadian machine-gunners dig in on their objective.

Continuing with the attack, by 7.30am the crest of Vimy Ridge was crossed by both brigades, and the western edge of Bois de la Folie – or what was left after the bombardment – was soon entered. On the front of the CMRs, the 8th Canadian Machine Gun Company had moved ahead of the infantry and were able to lay down protective fire while the CMRs came up. The 2nd CMR took the rubble of La Folie Farm, whilst the orchards reached by units of 7th Brigade were the scene of heavy fighting and several German counter-attacks. However, the Red Line was reached and a defensive flank established on the left by Royal Canadian Regiment and the 42nd Battalion.

With the Red Line now reached by three of the four divisions (the actions of 4th Division will be discussed later), the next phase was for 1st and 2nd Divisions to move on the Brown Line. Lipsett's men held fast in the Bois de la Folie, while 1st, 3rd and 4th Battalions of the 1st Division came up to the *Zwischen-Stellung*. From here they attacked the Blue Line with the leading waves,

> ...*advancing as if on parade, met remarkably little opposition, and casualties came mainly from shellfire.*[11]

Burstall's 2nd Division advance was led by 28th, 29th and 31st Battalions, with the British 13th Brigade (which had been held in reserve) on their left flank at the Bois de Goulot. Private Donald Fraser of the 31st Battalion (Alberta) recalled,

> *We were now near the crest of the ridge and a splendid view was obtained of the right. Our 1st Division and the adjoining Scottish Division were making very fine progress. In extended order with few blanks they were following close behind a rolling barrage. The barrage showed up as a wall of smoke and so perfect were the shells laid down that there were no gaps and the line was kept straight as*

Private Donald Fraser (NAC).

> *a die... It showed the artillery at their very best. The movable wall of bursting shells outlined by smoke was a pretty sight to watch.*
>
> *After a halt at the sunken path, we went forward on the heels of the 27th Battalion who were to complete the objective... Before us are broad lines of barbed wire hardly touched, a striking contrast to the wire we had already passed.... After*

waiting for a while the barrage showed signs of lifting and we truck ahead again... A perfect panorama enfolded before our eyes. The wide Douai plain stretched to the horizon devoid of woods. Nestling below the ridge was Farbus, Vimy and further north Givenchy and Lens. Beyond Farbus was Willerval and on the horizon could be discerned several more villages.[12]

The Blue Line was reached by both formations and the planned halt took place before an attempt was made to continue to the final objective, the Brown Line. At this point the weather changed for the better. Snow and sleet gave way to sunshine; but as the afternoon went on the sleet returned along with the cold. But to all Canadians present on this part of the battlefield it was clear – the Ridge was all but won.

For the attack on the Brown Line, the 1st Brigade were on the right, 27th and 29th Battalions in the middle, and the British 13th Brigade, with 1st Royal West Kents and 2nd King's Own Scottish Borderers on the left. The uncut wire noticed by Fraser had been expected and in the 1st Brigade soldiers equipped with wire cutters went forward to make paths for the infantry while the barrage suppressed the German trenches. This enabled them to reach Farbus Wood but in the Bois de La Ville the 27th and 29th Battalions were coming under fire from machine-guns and 77mm field guns firing at point blank ranges into their ranks, in most cases direct from

MkII tanks advance to support the Canadian attack.

their gun pits. Both battalions charged downhill, and these positions were soon over-run at the point of the bayonet, with the commander of the 3rd Bavarian Reserve Regiment being among the prisoners and nine guns taken in the process. The two British battalions had taken all their objectives and at the close of operation were consolidating and mopping-up their newly won positions in the Brown Line at Bois de Goulot.

With the Brown Line in Canadian hands, an attempt to exploit the situation was made by a unit of the Canadian Cavalry Brigade. Most commanders saw Vimy Ridge as a limited objective; take the Ridge and hold it. But some saw otherwise, and several cavalry units were

28

German dug-outs in Farbus Wood.

Captured German gun positions in Farbus Wood, April 1917.

827

held ready to exploit any situation that arose. With the Brown Line in their hands, Byng ordered a cavalry patrol to move on Willerval. At 4.20pm two patrols from the Canadian Light Horse cantered down the Thélus-Willerval road.

> One patrol captured ten Germans in the village, but in turn was engaged by a machine-gun and lost half its men and horses; the other was all but wiped out by rifle fire. The main body of the squadron was shelled and half its horses were killed.[13]

It was a somewhat inglorious end to the events on the right flank, but nothing could take away the achievement of these three Canadian divisions. Events to the north, from Hill 145 to The Pimple, were somewhat different.

Hill 145, as the name suggests 145 metres above sea level, dominated the crest of Vimy Ridge. From here the Germans could see into the Canadian rear, in particular the Souchez and Zouave Valleys. While the view enjoyed by the enemy was significant, the Canadian Corps realised from the study of maps alone that the view from Hill 145 across the Douai Plain would be even more impressive – and would enable them to dominate this part of the battlefield. The Germans were clear about this as well, and as such the defences around this position were amongst the strongest faced by Byng's men:

> The German First Line here consisted of two trenches; the round summit of the hill itself was ringed with two more... and on the reverse slope a system of deep dug-outs (the Hangstellung) housed the reserve companies.[14]

The hill was to be assaulted by Brigadier General V.W. Odlum's 11th Brigade of the 4th (Canadian) Division, with Brigadier General J.H.

MacBrien's 12th Brigade advancing on the left flank, covering the ground to the north, towards The Pimple. It had been hoped to overrun the forward positions in a surprise attack, but the view enjoyed by the defenders, even under a terrific bombardment, made this impossible. Instead the men would follow a creeping barrage to the objectives. In the first wave of 11 Brigade was the 102nd Battalion.

When at the stroke of 5.30am the barrage opened, a driving snow was falling. It was just light enough to see, and within five minutes observers came down to report that the men of the 102nd had gone over as one man in perfect formation.[15]

By 6am reports came back that the second line positions had been taken, and forty minutes afterwards news that the third line was won. In the meantime, the German positions around the Broadmash Crater had been outflanked, and a strongpoint there taken. Casualties, however, were heavy, particularly amongst the officers. In the forward area of the battlefield, all the officers were killed or wounded, and command had passed to Company Sergeant Major J. Russell of C Company, until he was also wounded. For his bravery in taking the initiative that day Russell was awarded the Distinguished Conduct Medal. He survived the war.[16]

On the left flank things were not going so well. On this part of the battlefield the barrage had not been so effective, and one section of trench had been virtually untouched. As the 87th Battalion (Grenadier Guards of Canada) began their advance here, they came under terrific machine-gun fire which cut down half of their leading assault wave, and pinned down the flank attack of the neighbouring 75th Battalion in their assembly positions.

The prized view across the Douai plain once Vimy Ridge had been taken.

Those who could pressed on, though harassed in flank and rear by machine-gun fire from the uncaptured sector, and from Germans who emerged from mine shafts and dug-outs after the leading wave had passed. Then came murderous fire from the second trench, whose garrison had been given ample time to man their positions.[17]

The 12th Brigade on the extreme left were also encountering problems. With three attacking battalions in the first wave, two mines had been blown at zero hour wiping out most of the opposition in front of the middle battalion, 73rd Battalion (Black Watch of Montreal). The first line trench was taken quickly and the 73rd then set about establishing a firm left flank. The 38th Battalion (Eastern Ontario) continued with the advance, but the ground proved hard going for the men, as the bombardment had smashed it to pieces. However, many dugouts in the German line had been untouched by the shells. At the entrance to one of these Captain T.W.MacDowell DSO confronted seventy-five Germans, tricking them into believing he was the advance guard of a more powerful force and getting them to surrender – when, in truth, he

only had two of his own men close by. For this plucky act, and several others that day, MacDowell was awarded the Victoria Cross. His citation reads:

For most conspicuous bravery and indomitable resolution in face of heavy machine-gun and shell fire. By his initiative and courage this officer, with the assistance of two runners, was enabled, in the face of great difficulties, to capture two machine-guns, besides two officers and seventy-five men. Although wounded in the hand, he continued for five days to hold the position gained, in spite of heavy shell fire, until eventually relieved by his battalion. By his bravery and prompt action he undoubtedly succeeded in rounding up a very strong enemy machine-gun post.[18]

Capt T.W.MacDowell VC DSO (NAC).

While this fighting was taking place on the left flank, further observation from the direction of The Pimple had been blocked by en effective smoke barrage and partially by the snow blizzard. However, the smoke had begun to disperse, and in the final push for the second and third lines, the men of 4th Division were under clear observation from this direction and came under withering machine-gun fire as a result. The 78th Battalion passed through Captain MacDowell and his comrades of the 38th, but only a handful made it to the objective. When they got there a strong force of Germans counter-attacked, and it was largely thanks to Lewis gun fire from the flanks that the position was held. Meanwhile the 85th Battalion had come up, and their commitment also aided the 54th Battalion to advance onto Hill 145 in support of the 102nd, still holding fast. By nightfall, while most of Hill 145 was in the hands of the Canadians, the position was precarious and many objectives were still eluding them. But the historian of the 54th Battalion summed up the feelings of many Canadians when he recalled the reaction on reaching the highest point of the Ridge,

> *It was a wonderful sight, when for the first time, we looked over the other side of the ridge after gazing at the top of it from our side for so many months. We were amazed to see a flat, open plain, and in the distance the city of Lens and the spires of Douai cathedral.*[19]

Hill 145 finally fell the next day, when elements of the reserve 10th Brigade came up and took the Red Line objectives. A second barrage of the ground above the Hangstellung proved effective, and an assault down the eastern slopes of the ridge on 10th April was led by the 44th and 50th Battalions. The 50th Battalion took over 240 casualties in this attack, and Private J.G. Pattison was awarded the final Victoria Cross for bravery in the attack on Vimy Ridge. Pattison was a Londoner who emigrated to Canada in 1906 and joined the Canadian forces in 1916, when he was forty years old. Vimy was his first battle. The citation for his VC reads:

Pte J.G.Pattison VC (NAC).

> *For most conspicuous bravery in attack. When the advance of our troops was held up by an enemy machine-gun, which was inflicting severe casualties, Pte Pattison, with utter disregard of his own safety, sprang forward, and jumping from shell-hole to shell-hole, reached cover within thirty yards of the enemy gun. From this point, in the face of heavy fire, he hurled bombs, killing and*

wounding some of the crew, then rushed forward, overcoming and bayoneting the surviving five gunners. His valour and initiative undoubtedly saved the situation and made possible the further advance to the objective.[20]

Pattison knew of the award of the VC, but never lived to wear it, being killed near Avion in June 1917.

By the afternoon of 10th April more than 7,000 yards of Vimy Ridge was in the hands of the Canadian Corps, with an advance to a maximum depth of 4,000 yards. On the right flank there had been the planned link up with elements of 51st (Highland) Division in the neighbouring XVII Corps (see Chapter 2) at the Brown Line positions. More than 3,400 prisoners had been taken. Byng's men now dominated the Douai Plain and the chances of a German counter-attack regaining the Ridge seemed improbable. But it had all come at a price; casualties in two days fighting amounted to 7,707 officers and men; some 2,967 of them fatal.[21] But one part of the ridge still remained in German hands – The Pimple.

The Pimple had been arguably the most active part of Vimy Ridge prior to the arrival of the Canadian Corps (see above). For the forthcoming attack on the Ridge, it had initially been the objective of British troops, but this was changed so that a secondary attack on the northern part of this section of the Ridge would follow the capture of the remainder of it by the rest of the Corps. The 10th Brigade of 4th (Canadian) Division was given the task, but they had been committed to the fighting on Hill 145 on 10th April, only returning to their rest area in Zouave Valley the next day. The weather prevented any further operations until the 12th April, when the 44th, 50th and 46th Battalions attacked from right to left. Supported by a strong bombardment, which included Livens projectors [22] of the Special Brigade, Royal Engineers (the first use of them in conjunction with Canadian troops), more than a hundred field guns opened up at 5am on the 12th.

The weather, in conjunction with the bombardment, proved effective. German machine-gunners were blinded by the driving snow and generally the defenders were not on a state of alert as they had not expected an attack in such conditions. These same conditions, most notably the mud, also affected the attackers. The bombardment soon got away from the assault waves, but despite this the 44th was established on the crest of The Pimple in just over an hour; the battalion's Lewis gunners cut down more than 100 Germans who were retreating towards Givenchy-en-Gohelle village. The 50th had taken the shattered stumps of Givenchy Wood and the 46th secured the left flank around the Souchez river. The last remaining Germans opposing the Canadians withdrew the next day.

Vimy Ridge had been taken. Vimy Ridge was now forever Canadian.

A Walk in the Canadian Corps Sector

This walks takes at least four hours (depending on the time spent in the Vimy Memorial Park). Cemeteries mentioned in bold are described in the section below.

Park your car at **Zouave Valley Cemetery**. This is reached from the main road (D937) in Souchez, by following the green CWGC signs to the cemetery. From here there are good views across the valley, towards The Pimple and the trees of the Memorial Park. Leave the cemetery and return along the minor road towards Souchez. On the outskirts of the village take the first road on the right. At the end turn right, and follow the road winding up the hillside. There is a good view back down Zouave Valley, and about half way up the hill, in a field to your right, is the remains of a British communication trench (probably Uhlan Alley) that once led to the front line positions on The Pimple.

Stay on this road. It goes under the motorway, and just past this tunnel take a minor road to your left. This then runs parallel with the motorway; follow to the end. Where the road finishes, ahead of you is a piece of pasture land. Go into this field (there is public access); sitting on a mound close to a line of scrubby trees to your right was the 44th Battalion memorial, finally demolished in 2005.

This memorial was one of the few original wartime unit memorials to survive into the twenty first century. It commemorates the men of

The 44th Bn CEF memorial in the Pimple shortly before demolition, 2005.

The memorial in 1918.

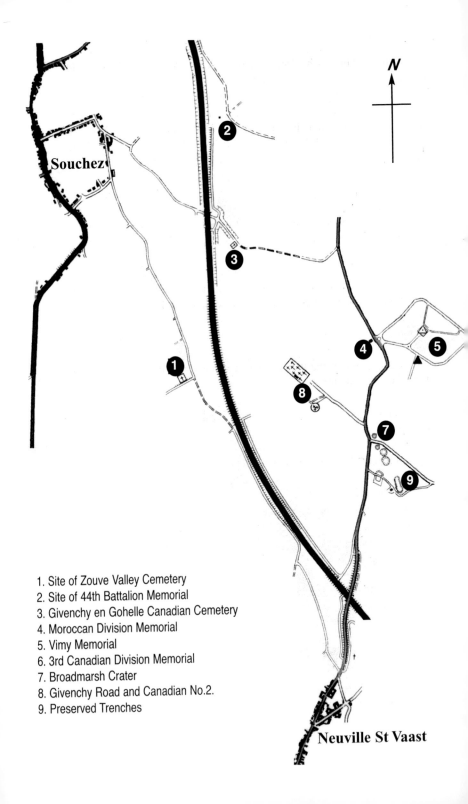

N

Souchez

1. Site of Zouve Valley Cemetery
2. Site of 44th Battalion Memorial
3. Givenchy en Gohelle Canadian Cemetery
4. Moroccan Division Memorial
5. Vimy Memorial
6. 3rd Canadian Division Memorial
7. Broadmarsh Crater
8. Givenchy Road and Canadian No.2.
9. Preserved Trenches

Neuville St Vaast

the 44th Battalion, who fought here in April 1917 – the legend '44 CANADA' which was on the concrete facings was visible to the end. The memorial was made during the winter of 1917/18, when the Canadian Corps returned to the area around Vimy Ridge. It was designed by Captain H.B. Rugh of the Battalion, who had been an architect in civilian life, and was built by a Sergeant Davis and the pioneer section. A cross was placed on the top, and wooden boards listing the casualties for the Vimy battle placed on the four sides. The 44th had a very strong Old Comrades Association, and in 1926 it was reported that,

> ... the monument raised by the 44th pioneers up on 'The Pimple' after the capture of Vimy Ridge, is to be demolished to make way for the Canadian Memorial.[23]

The Old Comrades Association acted quickly, and raised funds to bring the cross and wooden boards back to Canada, where they became part of a new memorial in St Jame's Park, Winnipeg. The memorial was unveiled by Mrs Bowes of Boissevan, who had lost three sons serving with the battalion.[24] But it took almost eighty years for the memorial to be finally demolished, a sad end to a silent witness, standing alone and almost forgotten by the thousands of Canadian visitors to Vimy Ridge less than a kilometre away.

Retrace your steps and rejoin the road you were on before. At the junction near the tunnel, turn left. Just past the sunken part of this road on the right is **Givenchy-en-Gohelle Canadian Cemetery**. Take time to visit this cemetery before proceeding along the track to where it joins the D55, Givenchy road.

This part of the battlefield is where units of 4th Division attacked on 9th April 1917. It is heavily wooded and signs of trenches and shell holes are visible amongst the trees. It was here that the 72nd Battalion advanced on the extreme left flank of the Canadian Corps, and where the 38th Battalion came up later; further down this track you will be close to the spot where Captain T.W. MacDowell DSO carried out the exploit which earned him his VC (see above). To their right the 87th Battalion attempted to advance, but were caught by enfilade fire from Broadmarsh Crater, which will be seen later in the walk.

At the D55, turn right and take this road into the Vimy Memorial Park. At the roundabout you will see the memorial to the French Moroccan troops who fought here in May 1915. It signifies the high-tide mark of the French advances of that year; the Colonials reached the lower slopes of Hill 145 only to be thrown back by a counter-attack. At the roundabout go straight over and head for the main area of the

The Vimy Memorial following its inauguration in 1936.

Vimy Memorial. Visit this area first.

In the years following the Great War the attack at Vimy came to symbolise the achievements and sacrifice of the Canadian nation in that conflict. Having lost more than 66,000 during the war, the Canadians were keen to commemorate them; all along the Western Front memorials were built on the spots where the Canadian Corps fought. However, they wanted one main focus for their remembrance, and the obvious place for that was Vimy; the place where for the one and only time in the Great War, all four Canadian divisions fought side by side. A section of the ridge was given to Canada by the French and plans unfolded to erect a memorial on the highest point at Hill 145. This memorial would jointly commemorate the capture of Vimy Ridge, and the Canadian soldiers who fell in France who have no known grave. Following a competition for the design, Toronto architect Walter S. Allward won, with a scheme that came to him in a dream. Work started in 1925, but the battlefields were a difficult place to build a memorial and it took nearly two years to construct the access road from Thelus. Foundations were then constructed, and in the process more than 15,000 tons of concrete and reinforcing rods were brought in for this purpose. The stone chosen for the memorial was Trau limestone from Dalmatia; six thousand tons were brought in and the memorial was finally complete by 1936. The names of more than 11,000 Canadian soldiers missing in France were carved on the walls at the base.

More than 10,000 Canadians came for the unveiling of the Vimy

metres to the memorial to the 3rd (Canadian) Division. This memorial, close to the site of La Folie Farm, is on ground taken by the 2nd and 4th Canadian Mounted Rifles of 3rd Division on 9th April 1917. Trenches and shell holes are still visible among the trees here.

Stay on the track and follow it to the main road. There is a path by the side of the road. Go right and follow this path to the next road junction. You will soon see the area of preserved trenches across to your left (visited shortly), and then a ride cut through the trees on your right looking back to the Vimy Memorial. Signs of mine craters are also visible and on the road junction a large crater can be see to the right of the road.

This is Broadmarsh Crater. An action was fought here on 21st May 1916 when the 8th Battalion Loyal North Lancs organised a counter-attack to recapture the crater following the fighting on this part of the Ridge a few days before. Lieutenant B.B. Jones was posthumously awarded a Victoria Cross for his bravery on this day. His citation reads:

For most conspicuous bravery. He was holding, with his platoon, a crater recently captured from the enemy. About 7.30pm the enemy exploded a mine forty yards to his right, and at the same time put a heavy barrage of fire on our trenches, thus isolating the platoon. They then attacked in overwhelming numbers. Lt Jones kept his men together, steadying them by his fine example, and shot no less than fifteen of the enemy as they advanced, counting them aloud as he did so to cheer his men. When his ammunition was expended he took a bomb, but was shot through the head while getting up to throw it. His splendid courage had so encouraged his men that when they had no more ammunition or bombs they threw stones and ammunition boxes at the enemy till only nine of the platoon were left. Finally they were compelled to retire.[27]

Jones' body was never recovered and he is today commemorated on the Arras Memorial. The Broadmarsh Crater remained in the hands of the Germans up until the attack on 9th April 1917, when machine-guns from it laid down withering fire in the flank attack of the Canadian Corps that morning.

At the junction turn right and continue on the path. Soon afterwards you will see a road on your left with a barrier. Follow this to **Givenchy Road Canadian Cemetery** and **Canadian Cemetery No 2**. Retrace your steps and return to the main road, and the path. Continue past the Broadmarsh Crater, and you will come to an entrance to a large parking area; enter here and head for the building you can see ahead.

All that remain of Neuville St Vaast in 1919.

This is the area of preserved trenches. It was decided that a section of the line should be preserved and it was felt the best way to do this was by using concrete; with concrete sandbags and duckboards. While this is all false, it does give a good impression of a forward area of the battlefield, in this case only separated from the enemy trenches by a mine crater. All these trenches and craters date from 1916/17, and the Royal Canadian Regiment and Princess Patricia's Canadian Light Infantry advanced from there on 9th April 1917. Nearby are toilets and the visitors' centre where you can request a free guided tour of the Grange Subway below this section of the ridge. The tour can take up to an hour, and can only be done in small groups. However, it does give you a good idea of the conditions under which the Canadians sheltered on the eve of the battle.

Return to the D55 and turn left in the direction of Neuville St Vaast. Cross over the motorway. Past the bridge in the fields on your left you may see two memorials to French soldiers killed here in 1915. Just before entering the village, take the first minor road on your right, which parallels the motorway and takes you across the fields and back to Zouave Valley Cemetery.

Associated Cemeteries
In 1917 most of the Canadian cemeteries in the Vimy area were given a number rather than a name by the Corps burial officer – usually

prefixed by a CC or CD. For example Bumble Trench Cemetery was CC 186. The first letter stood simply for the 'cemetery'. The second denoted which division made the cemetery: A for 1st Division, B for 2nd Division, C for 3rd Divisions and D for 4th Division. Where this information is known I have included it in the details of the cemetery.

ARRAS ROAD CEMETERY, ROCLINCOURT

Arras Road Cemetery is on the west side of the main road from Arras to Lens, north of Roclincourt village. It was started by the 2nd Canadian Infantry Brigade soon after the 9th April 1917 and until the end of the war it only contained the graves of seventy-one officers and men of the 7th Battalion (British Columbia Regiment) who fell in April to June 1917. These graves are now at the back of the cemetery, but in 1926-29, the cemetery was enlarged by the concentration of 993 graves from a wide area. This was mainly north and east of Arras, but also from as far away as Loos and the Franco-Belgian border. It now contains the graves of 923 British soldiers, 111 Canadians, twenty-two Australian, one New Zealand and one unidentified German soldier. The unnamed British graves are 802 in number, or nearly four-fifths of the whole.

Private L. Singh (III-O-26) is possibly a unique Canadian casualty of the Great War. He was killed with the 75th Battalion on 24th October 1918, and was part of the small Indian Sikh community that existed in Canada before 1914. He is the only known member of that community to be killed with the Canadians. Although not connected

The Canadian Corps artillery memorial at Thelus in 1919.

with the subject of this book, another important grave here is that of Captain A.F.G. Kilby VC MC (III-N-27), who was killed with the 2nd South Staffordshire Regiment at Loos on 25th September 1915. The citation for his posthumous award reads:

For most conspicuous bravery. Captain Kilby was specially selected at his own request, and on account of the gallantry which he had previously displayed on many occasions, to attack with his Company a strong enemy redoubt. The Company charged along the narrow towpath, headed by Captain Kilby, who, though wounded at the outset, continued to lead his men right up to the enemy wire under a devastating machine gun fire and a shower of bombs. Here he was shot down, but, although his foot had been blown off, he continued to cheer on his men and to use a rifle. Captain Kilby has been missing since the date of the performance of this great act of valour, and his death has now to be presumed.[28]

BOIS CARRÉ BRITISH CEMETERY, THÉLUS

Located close to Bois Carré ('square wood') in the village of Thélus, the cemetery was started by units of the 1st (Canadian) Division who advanced through here on 9th April 1917. It remained in use until June by which time there were sixty-one graves, which now form Plot I. After the war 425 graves were moved in from the surrounding battlefields, the final burial being a Canadian soldier accidentally killed clearing the battlefields in 1919. A Casualty Clearing Station opened nearby in 1940 and six graves were also added in the Second World War. Burials total: 371 Canadians and 116 British. There are fifty-nine unknowns and fifteen Special Memorials.

The following cemeteries were among those concentrated into Bois Carré after the war:

BUMBLE TRENCH CEMETERY, VIMY (CC 186): Located on the main road from Vimy to Lens, before the railway crossing. Here were buried, in May-August 1917, nineteen Canadian soldiers and five British.

CANADIAN GRAVE CD2, NEUVILLE ST VAAST: This was located 2,000 yards west of Petit Vimy, and forty-eight men of the 54th and 102nd Battalions who fell on 9th April 1917 were buried here. They were soldiers who had been killed in the fighting on Hill 145.

VIMY STATION CEMETERY: Where seventeen Canadian soldiers were buried in April – May 1917.

From the April 1917 fighting, casualties from the PPCLI, 42nd, 54th and 102nd Battalion dominate the burials. Major J.L. Dashwood MC (V-A-14) is the most senior Canadian buried here. He was killed on 13th April 1917. He had been decorated for bravery for a trench raid leading up to the attack on Vimy. Some of the British troops attached to the Canadians are also found in this cemetery; there is a row of 1st Royal West Kents and others found scattered here and there in the cemetery.

One interesting feature of this cemetery is the large number of men from the Royal Flying Corps found among the burials, largely killed during 'Bloody April' of 1917. Among them are two victims of the 'Red Baron', Manfred von Richtofen: Second Lieutenant Guy Everingham (III-B-13) and Second Lieutenant Keith Ingleby MacKenzie (III-B-12). They were the crew of a BE2G from 16th Squadron RFC who were shot down over Vimy on 8th April 1917 while observing for the opening barrage and were Von Richtofen's thirty-ninth victory. MacKenzie was the pilot, and Everingham the observer; the latter had come up from the ranks, and had served with the Royal Welsh Fusiliers on the Somme in 1916. Tragically, Everingham had only married on 19th February 1917.

Close to this cemetery, up a track from the main road, is the memorial to the 1st Canadian Division, originally erected in December 1917, following the capture of the ridge.

CANADIAN CEMETERY No 2, NEUVILLE ST VAAST

This cemetery, also in the boundary of the Vimy Memorial Park, was started following the capture of the Ridge in April 1917; casualties from 4th (Canadian) Division being amongst the first burials. A large number of graves were moved into the site after the war, and the cemetery was reopened as a main concentration cemetery for the Arras area in 1931, with the last major burials taking place in 1947, although a few have been added since. Burials total: 2,232 British, 641 Canadian, nineteen Australian, seven New Zealand, two South African, two Newfoundland and one Indian. Of the British burials over seventy percent are unknowns, and there are sixty-two Special Memorials.

Most of the Canadian dead are men from the 87th Battalion cut down in No Man's Land on 9th April 1917, and of the 75th Battalion hit by enfilade fire from the north of Hill 145.

The Cabaret Rouge canteen, close to the cemetery, in 1928.

CABARET ROUGE BRITISH CEMETERY, SOUCHEZ
Cabaret Rouge was the name given to a small building alongside the
Arras road, at a place known locally as Le Corroy. The cemetery was
established here by British units in 1916 and remained in use until
August 1917, and then again at intervals until September 1918; most
graves were from the 47th (London) Division and Canadian units.
These burials now form Plots I to V. After the war it was chosen to be
the main concentration cemetery for this area of France and many
thousands of isolated graves and dozens of small cemeteries were

Cabaret Rouge British Cemetery in the late 1920s.

closed and moved in here. Burials are now: 6,727 British, 749 Canadian, 116 Australian, forty-three South African, fifteen Indian, seven New Zealand and four German. This total of 7,661 (of which 4,487 are unidentified) makes it the largest cemetery on the Arras battlefield and one of the largest in Northern France.

Until recently two of the most visited Canadian graves here were the Chenier brothers. Privates Oliver (XII-E-16) and Wilfred (XII-E-15) were killed side by side serving with the Royal Canadian Regiment on 9th April 1917. They were from Buckingham, Quebec. In May 2000 the Canadian authorities, with the permission of the Commonwealth War Graves Commission, exhumed an unknown Canadian soldier from V111-E-7. This was part of 'Operation Memoria', to take an unknown Canadian from World War One to become Canada's Unknown Soldier. This task was completed, and he now rests in an honoured tomb at the Peace Tower at Ottawa; a special headstone commemorates the event in the cemetery.

ÉCOIVRES MILITARY CEMETERY, MONT ST ELOI
Mont-St. Eloi (or Mont St Eloy) is a small village five miles north-west of Arras in the back area for British and Canadian troops in 1917. Thousands of soldiers were billeted here during the war, and its streets were the scene of a famous fist-fight between men of the 51st (Highland) Division and Canadians on the eve of the Battle of Vimy Ridge! The village stands on high ground overlooking the battlefields of Vimy and Souchez and the main Bethune-Arras road, and the ruined towers that rise from the nearby abbey (still standing) were used as an observation post during the French attacks on Neuville-St. Vaast and Givenchy in May, 1915, and again when the British were here; an RFC (and later RNAS) airfield was located in the ground below them. Close to Mont St Eloi is Écoivres, a hamlet lying at the foot of the hill, to the south-west, and about a mile from Mont-St. Eloi. Three cemeteries in the commune were used by the British troops who took over this front in March 1916: Bray Military Cemetery, Mont-St. Eloi Military Cemetery, and Écoivres Military Cemetery. Eight men of the 51st (Highland) Division were buried by the 153rd Brigade in March 1916, in a little group of graves known afterwards as Bray Military Cemetery, due south of the Mount, between the hamlet of Bray and the Bois de Maroeuil. These graves were moved after the war to Plot VIII, Row A, at Écoivres. Mont-St. Eloi Military Cemetery was nearly a mile north of the village, on the north-eastern edge of the Bois des Alleux. It was made by the French Tenth Army, who buried about 950 men in it, and

The abbey of Mont St Eloi in 1915.

was used in March 1916, for the burial of eight British and three Australian soldiers. In 1920 the French authorities brought in from a spot two miles to the east the remains of five men of the Royal Field Artillery who died in March 1917. These sixteen graves have since been moved to Cabaret-Rouge British Cemetery, Souchez (see above).

Écoivres Military Cemetery is really the extension of the Communal Cemetery and lies on the edge of the hamlet of Écoivres. The French Army had buried over 1,000 men in the Communal Cemetery and in three new plots to the south of it. The 46th (North Midland) Division took over use of the extension in March 1916, and their graves are in Rows A to F of Plot I. Successive divisions used the French military tramway to bring their dead in from the front trenches, and from the first row to the last buried them almost exactly in the order of date of death. The operations of the 25th Division on Vimy Ridge in May 1916 is recalled in Plots I and II. The 47th (London) Division burials (July to October, 1916) are in Plot III, Rows A to H. Canadian graves are an overwhelming majority in the rest of the Cemetery; Plots V and VI containing the graves of men who fell in the capture of Vimy Ridge (April, 1917). Near the entrance of the Communal Cemetery the 29th Canadian Infantry Battalion erected a memorial cross to eighty-five of their officers and men. Of the 1,735 graves in the British part of this Cemetery, 891 are those of soldiers from the United Kingdom; 828 are Canadian, four South African, and two Australian. Ten are those of German Prisoners of War.

There are many interesting and important Canadians buried at Écoivres. One tragic story involves the Stokes family from London, England. Young Stanley had emigrated with his father Horace to Canada before the war. They had both joined up in 1915, and served in the 1st Battalion from 1916. Stanley was killed on Vimy Ridge on 9th April 1917, aged sixteen. His father found the body on the battlefield and brought him back to Écoivres for burial (VI-E-3). But the war was to claim him, too, some months later – Horace was killed on 19th September 1917, aged forty, and is buried in Aix-Noulette Communal Cemetery Extension, only a few miles away (I-T-2). Captain Victor Gordon Tupper MC (V-D-10), commanded No 3 Company of the 16th Battalion (Canadian Scottish). He had been awarded the Military Cross for bravery as a signals officer in the fighting at Regina Trench, on the Somme. He was also the son of the Hon. Sir Charles Hibbert Tupper, KCMG, and Lady Tupper, of Vancouver, British Columbia and the grandson of Canadian Prime Minister Charles Tupper. He was killed leading his men on 9th April 1917, aged twenty-one.

GIVENCHY-EN-GOHELLE CANADIAN CEMETERY, SOUCHEZ

The cemetery was started during the fighting for Vimy Ridge by the Corps burial officers and was originally known as 'C.D.20'. The men were laid to rest among the former German positions, and it remained in use until the following month. Two more graves were added in March 1918 and burials total: 144 Canadian, eight British, and two whose unit is unknown. Of these, some twenty-eight are unidentified and there are fifteen Special Memorials.

Most of the dead are from 4th (Canadian) Division, killed in the fighting here on 9th April 1917. The 38th, 72nd and 73rd Battalions are particularly well represented. However, there are some earlier casualties here, too, and these must have been men whose remains were found once this ground had been captured on 9th April; among them is Rifleman A.J. Bray of the London Irish Rifles, who was killed on 22nd May 1916 (B-16).

GIVENCHY ROAD CANADIAN CEMETERY, NEUVILLE ST VAAST

Located in the grounds of the Vimy Memorial Park, this battlefield cemetery was originally called CD1 and contains the graves of 111 Canadians. Two are unknown, and all were killed on 9th April 1917. The majority are men from units in the 4th (Canadian) Division, with a high proportion from the 54th and 102nd Battalions who fell in the fighting for Hill 145.

LA CHAUDIÈRE MILITARY CEMETERY
La Chaudiere Military Cemetery is on the western side of the road from Arras to Lens, and north of Vimy village. The Cemetery was made at the foot of the Ridge, on the further (north-eastern) side, next to a house which had contained a camouflaged German gun position. It remained very small until, in the summer of 1919, it was used, under the name of Vimy Canadian Cemetery No 1, for the concentration of many other small graveyards and isolated graves made by the troops on or near the Ridge. Among the Cemeteries moved were:

ANNAPOLIS CEMETERY (CC 118): A group of fifty-two Canadian graves at the Bois de la Chaudière.

SUMACK CEMETERY (CD 19): Sometimes known as Gables Cemetery, it was close to Annapolis, containing thirty-nine Canadian and three British graves.

CHINOOK CEMETERY (CD 31): Located on the western side of the main road, half a mile north of La Chaudière, containing thirty-three Canadian and six British graves.

38th CANADIAN CEMETERY (CD 16): A little north-west of La Chaudière, containing sixteen Canadian graves and seven of the 16th Royal Warwicks (Birmingham Pals).

AVION BRITISH CEMETERY (CD 33): Also known as The Sandpits, it was a group of twenty Canadian and three British graves in the woods west of Avion.
Among the isolated graves found were those of several men of the 8th Border Regiment who fell in the 1916 fighting. The Cemetery contains the graves of 458 identified and 132 unidentified Canadian soldiers, ninety soldiers of units from the United Kingdom, and 184 unidentified soldiers (of whom some were probably Canadian). In addition it has memorials to six British and three Canadian soldiers, whose graves must be among the unidentified, and to three Canadians,

DISCOVER MORE ABOUT HISTORY

Pen & Sword Books now offer over 3,000 titles in print covering all aspects of history including Military, Maritime, Aviation, Local, Family, Transport, Crime, Political and soon Social History. We also do books on nostalgia and have now introduced a range of military DVD's and Historical Fiction. If you would like to receive our catalogues and leaflets on new books and offers, please fill in the details below and return this card [no postage required]. Alternatively, register online at www.pen-and-sword.co.uk.

[Please note: we do not sell data information to any third party companies.]

Title ...... Name..

Address..

.... Postcode......................

Email Address ....

If you wish to receive our email newsletter, please tick here

Visit www.WarfareMagazine.co.uk for free military history content including commemorative anniversary articles, military news, reviews, competitions and new product releases.

Website: www.pen-and-sword.co.uk • Email: enquiries@pen-and-sword.co.uk

Pen & Sword Books
FREEPOST SF5
47 Church Street
BARNSLEY
South Yorkshire
S70 2BR

whose graves in Sumack Cemetery were destroyed in subsequent fighting.

The Canadian graves from the April 1917 fighting are largely from the 3rd and 4th Divisions. Among the burial is Private J.G. Pattison VC (VI-C-14), 5th Battalion (Alberta Regiment), who was awarded the medal for the fighting on 10th April 1917 (see above). Pattison was later killed on 3rd June 1917 in the heavy fighting for the electrical generating station near Eleu. Private G.H. Packer (IV-E-12) of the 72nd Battalion died on 28th May 1917, aged thirty-nine. The register records, "... Lived in O'Kanagan Mission, British Columbia, and was game warden at the time of enlistment. Born at Barbados". One of the many Americans serving with the Canadians is also buried here. Lance Corporal R.F. Endress (X-B-3) was killed on 9th Aril 1917, aged twenty two, while serving with the Royal Canadian Regiment. From Detroit, Michigan, he had crossed to Canada in 1914 and joined the American Legion with many other Americans, ashamed that their country had not entered the war on the side of the Allies and who wanted to do their bit.

LA TARGETTE BRITISH CEMETERY (AUX RIETZ), NEUVILLE ST VAAST

La Targette is a small village on the road to Arras and was captured by French troops in the fighting here in May 1915. When the British took over Vimy Ridge, La Targette was used as a billet for troops going in and out of the line on Vimy Ridge, many caves in the area being used for this purpose. An Advanced Dressing Station was established and this remained in use well beyond the capture of the Ridge in April 1917. It remained in use until September 1918, and sixteen isolated graves from the village were added after the war. Burials now total: 332 British, 298 Canadian, three South African and three Indian. Among them are forty-one unknowns.

Many of the graves here are from artillery units; both Canadian and British artillery units had their gun sites close to La Targette. Among these is Major S.H. Doake DSO (I-J-1), who was killed serving with 52nd Brigade Royal Field Artillery on 30th March 1918, aged twenty-five. Doake had been a pre-war regular officer, being commissioned in 1912, and had served continuously in France and Flanders since August 1914. There are two brothers buried here: Drivers F. Sheridon (I-K-25) and M. Sheridon (I-K-24) were from Southwick, Sunderland. They were both killed on 28th May 1918, while serving with the same artillery unit as Major Doake, 52nd Brigade RFA.

LICHFIELD CRATER, THÉLUS

Lichfield Crater was a mine crater in the old No Man's Land, between Neuville St Vaast and Thelus, in an area where 2nd (Canadian) Division fought on 9th April 1917. The Canadian Corps burial officer buried fifty-two Canadians and one British soldier here in what was called CB 2A. In addition there are four whose unit is not known and one Russian soldier. The unidentified number sixteen and include the Russian. The only headstone is that of the British soldier, whose body was found on the lip of the crater after the war. The cemetery is round – the shape of the crater – with the names of those buried here listed on a wall at in front of the Cross of Scarifice.

The majority of the casualties buried here are from 4th Canadian Infantry Brigade (18th, 19th, 20th and 21st Battalions). They are buried close to where they fell on 9th April. Among them is Lance Sergeant E.W.Sifton VC of the 18th Battalion, awarded a posthumous VC on 9th April 1917 (see above for his citation).

NINE ELMS MILITARY CEMETERY, THÉLUS

Nine Elms was the name given to a group of trees some 500 yards east of the Arras-Lens road, between Thélus and Roclincourt. The cemetery was started after the advance on 9th April 1917, when eighty men of the 14th Battalion (Royal Montreal Regiment) were buried here in what is now Plot I, Row A. Further graves were added until June 1917, and three burials made in Plot I, Row C in July 1918. After the war 499 British and 231 French burials were brought in from the surrounding battlefields and the following cemeteries were closed and move in here:

ARRAS ROAD CEMETERY, THÉLUS: Located on the roadside a little north of Nine Elms Cemetery. Originally called CA 39, it contained the graves of forty-six Canadians, of whom thirty-nine belonged to the 15th Battalion who fell on 9th April 1917.

GRAVE CA 26, ROCLINCOURT: By the roadside a little south of Nine Elms, where seventy-two men from the 5th Battalion who fell on 9th April 1917 were buried.

GRAVE CA 35, NEUVILLE ST VAAST: Some 1,000 yards west of Nine Elms, where another twenty-three soldiers from the 15th Battalion were laid to rest after the fighting on 9th April.

GRAVE CA 40, THÉLUS: Located 300 yards west of the Arras-Lens road, by a light railway track. The 16th Battalion (Canadian Scottish) buried forty-four of their dead from 9th April here.

GRAVE CB 10, THÉLUS: 300 yards west of the hamlet of Les Tilleuls where fifty-two British soldiers were buried in April and May 1917.

GRAVE CC 3, VIMY: Just south of the highest point of the Ridge, in which were buried fifty-eight Canadians who fell on 9th/10th April 1917.

ROCLINCOURT SQUARE CEMETERY: Sometimes also called Roclincourt Forward Cemetery No 5, it was 1,100 yards north-west of the village of Roclincourt and has twenty-three burials from the 51st (Highland) Division who fell on 9th April 1917.

SEAFORTH CEMETERY, ROCLINCOURT: Also known as Roclincourt Forward Cemetery No 4, it was located a little north-west of the Square Cemetery (above). The 1/4th Seaforth Highlanders from 51st (Highland) Division buried twelve men who fell on 9th April here.

Burials on this site now total: 484 Canadian, 145 British, and fifty four French (177 French graves were removed after 1918). The unnamed British graves are 149, with fifty-five Special Memorials.

THÉLUS MILITARY CEMETERY

Burials were first made on this site in April 1917, when the Canadian Corps burial officer made CB8, which now forms Plot II. These were casualties from the 2nd (Canadian) Division who fell in the attack on Thélus. This cemetery remained in use until 1918, with the further plots being made between June 1917 and September 1918. After the war seventy-five graves were moved in from the surrounding area. Burials total: 245 Canadian, fifty British, and one German. Of these thirty-four are unknown.

Two brothers are buried in this cemetery. Sergeant Albert Denis (I-E-5) and Private Henri Denis (I-E-4) were French Canadians from Montreal, and were both killed on 24th September 1917 serving with the 22nd Battalion. RSM F.W. Hinchcliffe MC (IV-A-10) was the Regimental Sergeant Major of 25th Canadians and was killed on 9th April 1917 leading his men forward. He was awarded the rare tribute for a Warrant Officer of a Military Cross for bravery in 1916.

VILLERS STATION CEMETERY, VILLERS-AU-BOIS

One of the furthest cemeteries from Vimy Ridge directly connected with the fighting there in 1917, Villers-au-Bois was were 2nd and 3rd Divisions had their headquarters during the fighting. Lieutenant

General Sir Julian Byng had his Corps HQ not far away in Camblain l'Abbé. A Casualty Clearing Station had been established in Villers-au-Bois as early as 1916, and the cemetery begun about that time, being first used by British troops serving on the Ridge. It remained in use until the end of the war, and afterwards only nineteen graves were moved in from the surrounding area. The French graves that dated from the earlier operations were removed in 1923. Total burials are: 1,009 Canadian, 169 British, twenty South African and thirty-two Germans. There are nine whose unit is not known.

The graves from the attack on Vimy Ridge are found in Plots V to X. At one time the 52nd Battalion erected a wooden memorial cross in the cemetery to their dead, but this was removed sometime between the two world wars. On 1st March 1917 the Canadian Corps organised a large scale raid on the Ridge, with heavy losses. Many of the men killed in this operation are buried here, among them the two battalion commanders killed. Lieutenant Colonel A.H.G. Kemball CB DSO (VI-E-1) commanded the 54th Battalion and had been decorated for bravery on the Somme. He had previously served as a Gurkha officer, and had retired from the Indian Army in 1910, when he came to Canada. Lieutenant Colonel S.G. Beckett (VII-D-1) of the 75th Battalion is buried close by.

ZIVY CRATER, THÉLUS

Zivy Crater, similar to Lichfield Crater (above), was a mine crater in No Man's Land on the south side of the main road from Thélus to Neuville St Vaast. Originally called CB1, there are fifty Canadians here, of whom two are unidentified, and three men whose unit is not known. The majority fell on 9th April 1917, with a few later on. Like Lichfield Crater, most are from the 4th Canadian Infantry Brigade and again the names are recorded on a panel near the Cross of Sacrifice rather than with individual headstones.

ZOUAVE VALLEY CEMETERY, SOUCHEZ

Zouave Valley was the name given to the long valley east of Souchez, the scene of bitter fighting in 1915 when French Zouave troops fought here. Once the line was established on the northern crest of Vimy Ridge at The Pimple, fighting units serving in these positions established a burial ground in the valley. The cemetery was started in May 1916 by units of the 2nd Division. It remained in use until June 1917, and from late 1916 onwards became solely used by the 4th (Canadian) Division after they arrived here from the Somme. Plot I was added after the war, when forty-two isolated graves from the area around Souchez and battlefields further north (including Loos) were moved in. Burials now total: 138 British, ninety eight Canadian, eight South African and one German. There are sixty six unknowns, and eleven Special Memorials.

Among the original burials are several men from 226th Field Company, Royal Engineers, killed on 21st May 1916 when the Germans assaulted The Pimple (Plot II Row G). A few days later, Sergeant Raymond Drew of the 22nd (Kensington) Bn Royal Fusiliers was killed on 24th May 1916, age 32. Born at Eton, where his father was an Assistant Master, Drew was a member of the Bombay, Burma Trading Company and enlisted in 1914. The Canadian graves are largely 1st Division men from when the Corps first took over this sector and 4th Division casualties in the period leading up to the attack on The Pimple. Many of the latter are from the 75th Battalion who died in a disastrous four battalion trench raid on Vimy Ridge on 1st March 1917 (Plot II).

1 Maude, A.H. The 47th (London) Division 1914-1919 (Amalgamated Press 1922) p.51.
2 ibid. p.53.
3 Hitchcock, F. Stand To! A Diary of the Trenches (1936) p.181-182.
4 Nicholson, G.W.L. Canadian Expeditionary Force 1914-1919 (Queens Printer, Ottawa 1964) p.245.
5 ibid. p.252.
6 Fetherstonhaugh, R.C. The Royal Montreal Regiment 14th Battalion CEF 1914-1925 (Gazette Printing Co 1927) p.145.
7 ibid. p.146.
8 PRO ZJ1: London Gazette 8th June 1917.
9 Nicholson op cit. p.254.
10 PRO ZJ1: London Gazette 8th June 1917.
11 Nicholson op cit. p.256.
12 Roy, R.H. The Journal of Private Fraser (Sono Nis Press 1985) p. 264-265.
13 Nicholson op cit. p.258.
14 ibid. p.259.
15 McLeod Gould, L. From B.C. To Baisieux: Being the Narrative History of the 102nd Canadian Infantry Battalion (Cusack Press 1919) p.49-50.
16 Russell was awarded the DCM in the London Gazette 16th August 1917. He settled in Vancouver after the war.
17 Nicholson op cit. p.259-260.
18 PRO ZJ1: London Gazette 8th June 1917.
19 Anon. Cinquante-Quatre: Being a Short History of the 54th Canadian Infantry Battalion (no date, Canada, c.1920s) p.15.
20 PRO ZJ1: London Gazette 2nd August 1917.
21 Nicholson op cit. p.261.
22 These were trench mortar weapons that fired large, sausage-shaped projectiles containing poison gas.

23 Russenholt, E.S. <u>Six Thousand Canadian Men. The History of the 44th Battalion Canadian Infantry 1914-1919</u> (Winipeg 1932).
24 Her sons were Donald Clifford Bowes, killed 28/10/17, commemorated Menin Gate. Frederick Arnold Bowes, died of wounds 08/03/17, buried Barlin Communal Cemetery Extension. James Lawrence Bowes, died of wounds 28/02/17, buried Villers Station Cemetery.
25 Hundevad, J. (Ed) <u>Guide Book of The Pilgrimage to Vimy and The Battlefields: July-August 1936</u> (Canada 1936) p.16.
26 Pte Thomas Alexander Kemp, 72nd Battalion, died of wounds 26th June 1917, aged 41. Husband of Rose Ann Kemp of Rowley, Alberta, Canada. Native of Alexandra Park, London, England. Villers Station Cemetery (IX-D-7).
27 PROJZ1: <u>London Gazette</u> 5th August 1916.
28 PRO JZ1: <u>London Gazette</u> 30th March 1916.

Wounded being evacuated on a narrow gauge railway.

Chapter 2

XVII CORPS: 34TH AND 51ST (HIGHLAND) DIVISIONS
9th/10th APRIL 1917

The Battle

Major General C.L. Nicholson's 34th Division had only been in the Arras sector for less than six weeks, having come down from Armentières in late February 1917. This Division had suffered heavily on the Somme the year before, when two of its brigade, comprised entirely of battalions of the Northumberland Fusiliers (the Tyneside Scottish & Irish), had been all but wiped out. Rebuilt with reinforcements from England, by the time of Arras some of those wounded on the Somme had returned and so several of the battalions retained something of their original character.

For the attack on 9th April 1917, 34th Division was holding a fairly narrow front, but with all three of its brigades in the line. Its front line rested on the Arras-Bailleul road on the right and the Roclincourt-

The German trench system near Roclincourt.

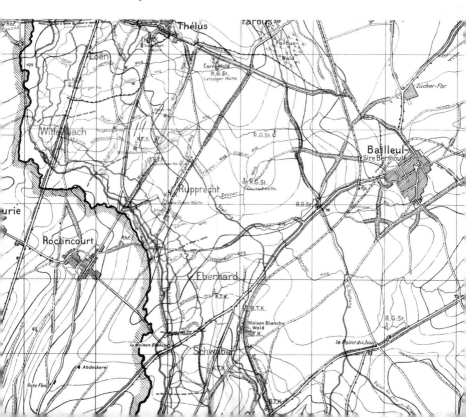

Bailleul road on the left where it joined with 51st (Highland) Division. The enemy positions opposite dated back to late 1914, and had been unaffected during the withdrawal to the Hindenburg Line. The initial objective was the Black Line, beyond that the Blue, most of which rested on the railway cutting on the Lens – Arras railway line; and the Brown Line ran from the Maison de la Côte on the Bailleul road to the Point du Jour on the Douai road. The final objective, the Green Line, was only a few hundred yards beyond this latter point, where the positions of the 34th Division would meet up with those of the 4th Division. A great deal of artillery was allocated to the Division, including Army Brigades and some from 17th (Northern) Division, then attached to the Cavalry Corps. The attack of all three brigades would be protected by a creeping barrage, while heavier guns would pound the German defences.

At Zero Hour Brigadier General R.C. Gore's 101st Brigade was on the extreme right flank of the Division's advance. 11th Suffolks (Cambridgeshire Battalion) and 16th Royal Scots (2nd Edinburgh) led the advance, with 10th Lincolns (Grimsby Chums) and 15th Royal Scots (1st Edinburgh) in reserve. As they crossed No Man's Land,

> *... the enemy's artillery fire was weak, and his rifle and*
> *machine-gun fire feeble, most of his men being caught in their*

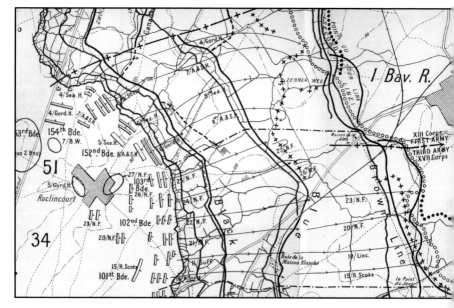

The Order of Battle for XVII Corps on 9th April 1917.

> *dugouts. His trenches were badly shattered, and the Black Line was occupied and consolidated without severe loss.*[1]

Indeed, the Suffolks had reached the Black Line without any casualties at all. Pushing on to the Blue Line in the area of the railway cutting somewhat heavier fire was received. The 16th Royal Scots,

> *... had their revenge on reaching the cutting, where they killed a number of the Boches and captured many others from the dugouts. One group of German machine-gunners fought to the death, and was only put out of action by a gallant charge led by 2nd Lieuts A.D.Flett and Thurburn, both of whom fell dead just before their men closed with the Boches.*[2]

While picking through some of the dugouts in the cutting, a party of men from the Battalion came across Captain Cowan, an officer of the 16th Royal Scots who had gone missing in one of the final trench raids made on the German lines on 7th April. Although wounded, he was alive and pleased to see his comrades who had all but given him up for dead.

At the Blue line 11th Suffolks and 16th Royal Scots consolidated, and 15th Royal Scots and 10th Lincolns were then to pass through en-route to the final objective. However, 15th Royal Scots had been unable to properly identify the Black Line, due to the heavy damage from the British barrage, and as such the men had pressed on and became inter-mingled with the forward parties of the advance. This

The dead of battle being removed for burial along the railway cutting near Bailleul.

meant that when the next leap forward was due from the cutting, the Royal Scots could only muster about 130 all ranks. Despite this they pressed on, the 15th Battalion taking its final objective just north of Point du Jour as a party of Germans approached them with hands up and carrying a white flag – only too willing to surrender.

The 10th Lincolns had a tougher time coming up on the left. Leaving the cutting they came under fire from some 77mm field guns beyond the Brown Line and intermittent sniper fire. However,

> ... *the companies pushed on until the wire in front of the Jimmy Line (formed by the Jewel and Jimmy trenches) was reached. This wire was ten feet wide and uncut. The men lay down whilst wire-cutting parties went forward to cut lanes. There was no opposition except from snipers, but by the time the wire was cut the barrage was far ahead, and the two leading companies were hopelessly mixed.[3]*

Despite this, once through the wire, the officers led the men to the final objective which was taken by 10th Lincolns without any serious opposition, but at the cost of three officer casualties; two of them mortally wounded. This was between 2pm and 2.30 and, although a counter-attack came later in the day, the position was held. Both 10th Lincolns and 15th Royal Scots would remain in these advanced positions for the next five days, until finally relieved.

The railway cutting near the Blue Line.

The centre attack was made by Brigadier General T.P.B. Ternan's 102 Brigade. This brigade comprised four battalions of Northumberland Fusiliers (20th-23rd), who were otherwise known as the Tyneside Scottish. The brigade had all but been annihilated on the first day of the Somme in 1916, but many of the wounded from that battle had now returned and were commanding companies, platoons and sections. This advance was in total contrast to July 1916, and was clear evidence of how the tactical approach to the war had changed and moved on. As the men from this Brigade advanced into the Black Line they discovered that the machine-gun barrage of the German positions had done its work. The intensity of the machine-gun fire was such that few of the defenders had dared to emerge from cover. Indeed, it was noted,

> ... the advance went like clockwork. Messages were regularly received and transmitted to Divisional Headquarters, giving the news of the fall of each of the enemy's trenches in succession, and the final objective, the enemy's last line on the extreme top of the slope was captured during the afternoon. Several batteries of the enemy's guns which they had been forced to abandon were also captured by the Brigade just over the top of the ridge... The capture of the top of the ridge entailed the retreat of the enemy for a considerable distance.[4]

The only major losses had been in the capture of the support line beyond the Blue Line objective, where the wire had not been cut and, as with the Grimsby Chums, the men of the Tyneside Scottish had been forced to lay down and cut lanes through it. Here alone they suffered some 165 casualties.[5]

The 103rd Brigade, commanded by Brigadier General H.E. Trevor, also consisted of four battalions of Northumberland Fusiliers but were known as the Tyneside Irish. They were the extreme left of 34th Division's advance, with 24th and 25th Battalions leading the attack and 26th and 27th to follow. It was to prove the most problematic part of the Division's advance on 9th April. While the Tyneside Irish took the first objective very quickly, capturing a large number of prisoners, in the advance on the Blue Line officer and NCOs casualties among the leading units were heavy. By the close of the day, for example, the 25th Battalion was down to only one officer and a handful of sergeants in two of its companies. On the left flank the attacking troops of the 51st (Highland) Division had failed to come up on time and, when they did arrive, had drifted south due to machine-gun fire and were mingled with troops of the 34th Division. This caused some confusion, and the

Mittel Weg trench now became crowded with men, but with few officers to lead them. However, Lieutenant Colonel Moutlon Barrett of the 25th Battalion sent a party forward to clear the Blue Line of machine guns. One of these parties contained Lance Corporal Thomas Bryan. Bryan was a Worcestshire lad, living near Leeds when the war broke out and a coal miner who had joined the Tyneside Irish as a reinforcement after their losses on the Somme in 1916. An officer of the party he was in later reported,

> ... Captain Huntley and L/Cpl Bryan had gone forward up a communication trench to see what they could do. Huntley was killed on the way up, while spying through his glasses. Bryan went on alone and killed the two gunners, so that the Blue Line was made safe for the other people who were to push on later in the day. The two witnesses said that they saw Bryan stab the two gunners – they saw his bayonet flashing. I saw the ground afterwards, and examined the machine-gun position. It had a wonderful field of fire, and had held up the brigades on our right and left. It had caught our people as they came over the ridge, about three hundred yards in front of the machine gun position. Our men and the men of the Scottish Division (on our left) were lying dead almost in a line, just on the ridge. But for Bryan, the division would never have reached its objective that day.[6]

Lance Corporal Thomas Bryan VC

For his bravery, Bryan was recommended for and awarded the Victoria Cross. His official citation in the London Gazette reads:

> For most conspicuous gallantry during an attack. Although wounded, this non-commissioned officer went forward alone, with a view to silencing a machine gun which was inflicting much damage. He worked up, most skilfully, a long communication trench, approached the gun from behind, disabled it, and killed two of the team as they were abandoning the gun. As this machine gun had been a serious obstacle in the advance to the second objective, the results obtained by Lance Corporal Bryan's gallant action were far-reaching.[7]

His VC was presented to him by the King on the field of the Newcastle United Football ground in June 1917; and although he returned to his

German barbed wire on the Bailleul road at the Blue Line.

battalion, Bryan survived the war and died in 1945.[8]

But further trouble was ahead. When the Tyneside Irish moved into the ground beyond the Blue Line they came under terrific machine-gun fire from the ruins of Maison de la Côte on the Bailleul road. This position dominated this part of the battlefield, and the Germans had fortified it with a large garrison armed with a number of Maxim guns. The Brigade Trench Mortar battery went forward to assist but on the 27th Battalion front,

> ... *Captain Neeves had organised the whole battalion, and worked round the left flank with Lewis guns along the Gaul Weg, and also on the right along the sunken road. They assaulted, but the enemy ran away. Our men were exhausted, owing to heavy going and bad weather... and could not catch them. The men entered the eastern Brown Line, and standing up, fired at the enemy running down the slope, and cheered lustily. Lewis guns did execution at long range.*[9]

During this action Private Ernest Sykes carried out a number of brave deeds that resulted in the award of the Victoria Cross. Sykes was a Yorkshireman who had worked on the railways before the war. He had originally served with the West Riding Regiment and been wounded with them at Gallipoli in 1915. He joined the 25th Northumberland Fusiliers (2nd Tyneside Irish) after the Somme, and was transferred to the 27th (4th Tyneside Irish) not long before Arras. On 9th April 1917, in the area of the Blue Line,

> ... *when his battalion in attack was held up about 350 yards in advance of our lines by intense fire from front and flank, and*

suffered heavy casualties. Private Sykes, despite this heavy fire, went forward and brought back four wounded – he made a fifth journey and remained out under conditions which appeared to be certain death, until he had bandaged all those who were too badly wounded to be moved. These gallant actions, performed under incessant machine-gun and rifle fire, showed an utter contempt for danger.[10]

Sykes received his VC from the King at Buckingham Palace, but joined Bryan in Newcastle where the city laid on a special reception for the two Arras heroes. Wounded after returning to the front, he was discharged in May 1918 and returned to his job on the railway. Sykes died in 1967.

To the north of 34th Division on 9th April 1917 was the 51st (Highland) Division commanded by the much respected Major General G.M. 'Uncle' Harper. Harper had commanded the Division since the Battle of Loos, and although the divisional flash, a red HD in a dark-blue circle, had led to the unit being referred to as 'Harper's Duds', the Jocks had proved their worth in the fighting at High Wood and the capture of Beaumont Hamel in 1916. For the attack at Arras, the Division had two brigades in the line. On the left 154th Brigade (Brigadier General J.G.H. Hamilton) had its flank on the Arras-Lens road and bordered with the Canadian Corps. On the right 152nd Brigade (Brigadier-General H.P. Burn) had the village of Roclincourt immediately behind it, with 34th Division on its flank. The Black Line objective was the area of the German front line, with the second objective on the Blue Line being at a roughly north-east direction from there and resting on the second line of defence. The final objective, the Brown Line, would be where the Division would meet with the Canadians on the left at the southern end of Vimy Ridge and 34th Division on the right, just short of Bailleul village. Before them were elements of the 1st Bavarian Reserve Regiment.

The 152nd Brigade attack was led with 6th Gordon Higlanders on the right and 6th Seaforth Highlanders on the left. The 6th Gordons reached their objectives on time and the Seaforths found their portion of the German line abandoned. A prisoner taken at this point,

... who had been head waiter in a hotel in the West End of London, told his captors that he knew of no troops behind the Blue Line, and that if they took this all would be easy.[11]

However, the 6th Seaforths thereafter experienced some heavy fighting in the next two objective lines. At one point the 5th Seaforths, coming up through them, found that the situation was far from resolved and had to join in the fighting and help clear and mop up the ground already won before they could continue with their own advance. Indeed, Brigadier-General Burns later recalled,

The 6th Seaforth Highlanders lost 326 officers and men in capturing the Black Line. One company of the 5th Seaforth Highlanders detailed to capture the Blue Line suffered 90 casaulties before reaching the Black Line. A second company... had used all its rifle grenades before reaching the Black Line. Only one officer of the 6th Seaforth Highlanders, detailed for the capture of the Blue Line, reached it. The remainder were all either killed or wounded.[12]

Two tanks had been detailed to assist the division in this advance, but both failed to arrive as they were put out of action before they reached the first wave of the assault. This was the second time Harper's men had been let down by the tanks; the last time had been at Beaumont Hamel in November 1916. The experience perhaps influenced Harper's approach to tanks for the rest of the war.[13] A final and unexpected event marked the capture of the final objective by 152nd Brigade.

As the troops for the Blue line were crossing the Black, an enormous explosion occurred. As a result a number of men were buried and several killed in both battalions. It was assumed that the Germans must have intentionally exploded a Minnenwerfer

Tanks advance to support the infantry assault, 9th April 1917.

bomb store, as shortly after the explosion six Germans voluntarily emerged from a dug-out. These men were assumed to have been responsible for this disaster, and were immediately killed.[14]

But finally, after eight hours of fighting, objectives were secured and contact was made with the formations on the Brigade's flanks.

In 154th Brigade, the fighting had also been severe. The Blue line had fallen, but with some loss. The 4th Gordon Highlanders in particular had taken heavy casualties at the Swischen Stellung, so much so that only two companies were left to continue to the next objective. On one part of the front a troublesome machine-gun was knocked out with the co-operation of an artillery officer, Capatin A.T. Saulez of D Battery, 64th Brigade Royal Field Artillery.

He observed from his observation post a German machine-gun in action at the junction of a communication trench and the Blue Line, holding off the infantry advance. He therefore telephoned to his own battery, and turned a selection of Howitzers from firing on the barrage on to the machine-gun. By this means he put the gun out of action, and enabled the infantry to continue their advance. Captain Saulez's shooting was admirable, and his action undoubtedly saved the infantry from many casualties.[15]

Sadly Saulez was killed later in the battle, and he does not appear to have been decorated for this action. It shows how much infantry-artillery co-operation had moved on since the start of the Somme battle in 1916, when a rigid and set bombardment would have made acts like this impossible.

By 1.40pm, elements from the Brigade had taken Tommy Trench and some five hours later the Brown Line was reached and the Jocks met up with the Canadian Corps on their left at a position known as the Commandant's House. It was thought that the entire Brown Line was now in the hands of the Division, until 5th Gordon Highlanders reported back that they could not make touch with the 154th Brigade on their left and that they were being fired on from this direction. The enemy, it seemed, was still in possession of part of this line. An attack by 7th Argyll and Sutherland Highlanders soon followed, which saw them attempting to bomb their way in, but this was held up by heavy machine-gun fire. The 5th Gordons tried to silence one of these guns on a small knoll close to the Brown Line, but this also failed and by now snow was falling heavily on the battlefield, making movement in the open conspicuous.

It took until the night of 11th/12th April for this part of the final objective to be taken. A Corporal from the 6th Gordons, one of the Divisional observers, reported back that,

> *… he had made his way into the Brown Line, and that it was unoccupied. He had found the electric light still burning in the dug-outs, packs and equipment neatly stacked, and unopened parcels, and unfinished meals lying on the tables.*[17]

With the Brown Line at last in their hands, the Division was relieved. Casualties had been heavy in some battalions, but the German formation defending the ground had been dealt a heavy blow, so much so that it gave up further ground just after the Highland Division pulled out. But for Harper's men, the bloody battle of Arras had only just begun.

A Walk in the 34th & 51st Divisional Sectors

This walk takes around 3¼ hours, and covers much of the area fought over by 34th and 51st (Highland) Division in the opening stage of the advance. It is a circular walk, starting and finishing at Roclincourt. Cemeteries referred to in **bold** are described below.

Park your vehicle next to **Roclincourt Military Cemetery**, in the heart of the village. The first part of the walk takes you across the ground fought over by 51st (Highland) Division on 9th April 1917.

The ruins of Roclincourt village.

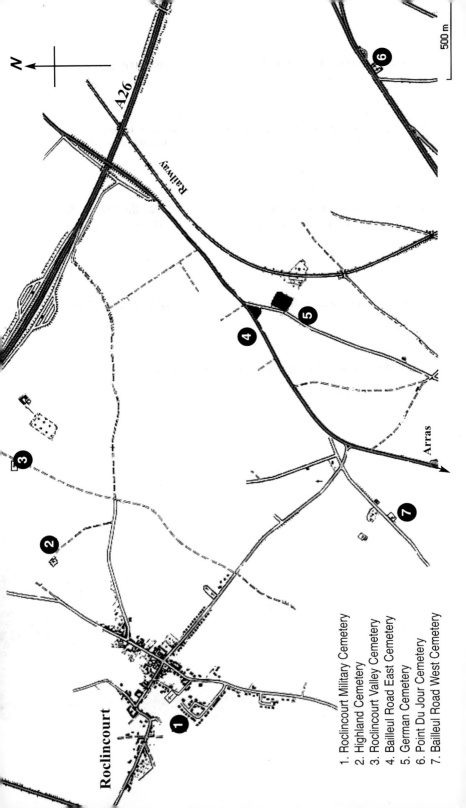

N

A26

Railway

Roclincourt

Arras

500 m

1. Roclincourt Military Cemetery
2. Highland Cemetery
3. Roclincourt Valley Cemetery
4. Bailleul Road East Cemetery
5. German Cemetery
6. Point Du Jour Cemetery
7. Bailleul Road West Cemetery

Take the minor road in front of the cemetery, down to the main road and turn left. Continue to the cross-roads and go straight across. On the outskirts of the village, take the first minor road on the right. After about 500 metres there is a path leading across the fields to **Highland Cemetery**. Return to the road, and turn left. Shortly afterwards you meet a junction of tracks; turn left and walk to **Roclincourt Valley Cemetery**.

Return to the junction and turn left. Here you are close to the boundary of 51st (Highland) and 34th Divisions and a good appreciation of the ground can be had from here. Take the next track on the right and follow it to the main road (D919). On this part of the walk you are close to the Blue Line, and near to where the 26th and 27th Northumberland Fusiliers were fighting and where Private Ernest Sykes got his Victoria Cross (see above).

At the main road walk carefully across to **Bailleul Road East Cemetery**. Looking west from the cemetery you have a good view across the ground attacked over by 101st and 102nd Brigade of 34th Division, with 11th Suffolks and 16th Royal Scots advancing close to where the cemetery is today. It is also close to the junction to where 9th

The Point du Jour.

(Scottish) Division advanced north of St Laurant Blangy.

After visiting the cemetery take the minor road alongside it to the **German Cemetery** at la Maison Blanche. This cemetery became one of two main German concentration cemeteries for this part of the Arras battlefield. More than 31,000 German soldiers are buried here. Leaving the cemetery turn left, and follow this minor road to a junction of tracks/roads; turn left and then left again and follow a track northeast to the railway line. There is a bridge across the railway line; from it, or on the track just beyond, you have a good view across the ground where the continuation of 34th Division's advance took place. The 10th Lincolns and 15th Royal Scots passed through this point, heading towards the Point du Jour. This ground is currently (mid-2003) being developed into an industrial area, and while it was once possible to walk to the 9th (Scottish) Division memorial on the main road, this may not be possible in the future.

It was also close to here in June 2001 that the Arras Archaeological Society unearthed the remains of more than twenty soldiers of the 10th Lincolns (Grimsby Chums) who had died in the early stage of the battle. The men were buried in a long trench grave, seemingly lying with linked arms – comrades in life, comrades in death. Unfortunately it proved impossible to identify any of the soldiers, but they were re-buried by the Commonwealth War Graves Commission at Point du Jour Cemetery on the eighty-fifth anniversary of the Battle of Arras.[18]

Retrace your steps, and go back to the cross-roads of tracks. Here go straight across on the track, which will take you across the fields to the D60. Here turn right, taking care on this busy road, and then take the next turning on the left, the continuation of the D60 and signposted

The mass grave of British soldiers found on the Pont du Jour.

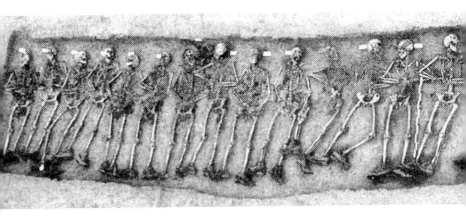

for Roclincourt. Then take the next minor road on the left, and follow to **Bailleul Road West Cemetery**. Returning to the D60, go left and follow back to Roclincourt and your vehicle.

<u>Associated Cemeteries</u>

BAILLEUL ROAD EAST CEMETERY
Bailleul Road East Cemetery was started by units of the 34th Division in April 1917, and remained in use by fighting units until November. Plot I, Row R, was added in August 1918 and Plots II, III, IV and V were made after the war by the concentration of isolated graves from a very wide area around Arras. Burials total: 1,225 British, forty-three Australian, twelve Canadian, six South African and one Newfoundland. Of these, more than 750 are unidentified, and there are seven Special Memorials to men once buried in Northumberland Cemetery, Fampoux, whose graves could not be found on concentration; and a number of graves in Plot V.

The following cemeteries were among those concentrated into this site after the war:

NORTHUMBERLAND CEMETERY, FAMPOUX: was on the west side of the road from Fampoux to Bailleul. This road was called Northumberland Lane, and a neighbouring trench was called Northumberland Avenue. The cemetery was used by fighting units from April to July 1917, and one other burial was made in it in September 1918. It contained the graves of sixty-nine British soldiers and these, with the exception of seven who were not found, were concentrated into Plot V of this cemetery.

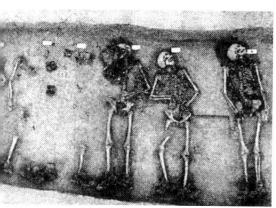

LAGNICOURT SOLDIERS CEMETERY: this was the German name for this cemetery, which was near the south-east side of the village of Lagnicourt. It contained the grave of one RFC officer who died in October 1916.

Probably the most visited grave in this cemetery is that of Private Isaac Rosenberg (V-C-12), the war poet. Rosenberg did not die in the 1917 battle, but was killed near Fampoux on 1st April 1918, aged twenty-seven, while serving with the 1st King's Own. Like many of those in this cemetery, Rosenberg was originally buried by the Germans in a mass grave, which was discovered after the war. In one of his finest poems, 'Returning, we hear the Larks', Rosenberg recalled that among the din of battle,

But hark! Joy – joy – strange joy.
Lo! Heights of night ringing with unseen larks:
Music showering on our upturned listening faces.

Death could drop from the dark
As easily as song –
But song only dropped...

More than eighty years later, the sound of larks can often be heard above the battlefields of Arras, here at Rosenberg's grave.

BAILLEUL ROAD WEST CEMETERY

This cemetery was started by the 12th Royal Scots in May 1917 and has ninety seven British graves. There are six unknowns, most of them from units in the 9th (Scottish) Division, and one South African. All died on the first day of the Battle of Arras.

HIGHLAND CEMETERY, ROCLINCOURT

Highland Cemetery is about half a mile north-east of the village of Roclincourt. Originally called Roclincourt Forward Cemetery No 1, it was made when the battlefields were cleared after the 9th April 1917. Plot I, Rows A and C, and Plot II, Rows A and D, are almost exclusively occupied by the graves of the 51st (Highland) Division who attacked here. Plot I, Row B and Plot II, Row C were made after the war, by the concentration of 114 graves from the battlefields around Arras. Among these in Plot II, Row C, are thirty graves of men from the Canadian Field Artillery and Canadian Railway Troops, brought here from Fond-de-Vase British Cemetery, nearly a mile east of Maroeuil. Burials total: 271 British, thirty-three Canadian, sixteen South African, one British West Indies Regiment and one completely unidentified soldier. There are forty-four unnamed graves, and one Special Memorial.

ROCLINCOURT VALLEY CEMETERY

The cemetery was started after the 9th April 1917 advance, also by the units of 51st (Highland) Division, which fought here on that day. It was used until the following August and it then contained the graves of ninety-four soldiers, of whom forty belonged to the Highland Division, and five French soldiers who had fallen in 1915; these French graves were removed in the 1920s. Plot I, Row F, was completed, and Plots II-IV made, after the war by the concentration of 455 graves from smaller cemeteries and from the surrounding battlefields. These graves are almost all from April 1917 and the majority of the soldiers buried in them belonged to the 34th and 51st (Highland) Divisions. Three of the wooden memorial crosses commemorating the Tyneside battalions were brought in at the same time, but they are no longer in the cemetery. Burials now total: 509 British, twenty-two South African, two Canadian, two New Zealand, with eighty-three unnamed graves; and there are four Special Memorials. The more important cemeteries concentrated into Roclincourt Valley Cemetery were the following:

KING CRATER CEMETERY, ROCLINCOURT: about a mile east of the village, in a mine crater far from any road. It contained five big graves, made by the 34th Division in the middle of April 1917; and in them were buried ninety-nine soldiers from the United Kingdom, all of whom fell on the 9th April and all but two of whom belonged to the Tyneside Brigades of the 34th Division.

KITE CRATER CEMETERY, ST LAURENT-BLANGY: nearly a mile south-east of Roclincourt village. It also contained five big graves, in which were buried fifty-three soldiers from the United Kingdom (largely from 34th Division), who fell on the 9th April 1917.

RABS ROAD CEMETERY, ST LAURENT-BLANGY: on the Arras-Bailleul road, a mile south-east of Roclincourt village. It contained the graves of twenty soldiers from the United Kingdom, sixteen of whom belonged to the 15th or 16th Royal Scots, and all of whom fell on the 9th or the 13th April 1917.

ROCLINCOURT LONG CEMETERY: called at one time Roclincourt Forward Cemetery No 3, it was located in a field three-quarters of a mile north of the village. The cemetery contained the graves of sixty-eight officers and men of the 51st (Highland) Division who fell on the 9th April 1917.

THÉLUS ROAD CEMETERY, ROCLINCOURT: located by the roadside nearly a mile north of the village. It was made by XVII Corps, and contained the graves of forty-two officers and men of the 51st (Highland) Division who fell here on the 9th April 1917.

ROCLINCOURT MILITARY CEMETERY

The French troops who held this front before March 1916 made a military cemetery (removed in the 1920s) on the south-west side of which a British Military Cemetery was made. It was started by units of the 51st (Highland) and 34th Divisions in April 1917 and contains many graves from the first day of the Battle of Arras. It remained in use as a front line cemetery until October 1918. After the war some fifty-one graves, mostly from the battlefield north of Roclincourt, were brought into Plot IV, Row F. Graves here total: 776 British, 134 Canadian, six whose unit could not be ascertained, and four German prisoners. Unknowns total thirty-three. During the war, the 22nd Royal Fusiliers (Kensingtons) erected a wooden memorial in the Cemetery to one officer and twenty-seven NCOs and men who fell in action at Oppy in April and May 1917. This was removed in the 1920s, and its current whereabouts is not known.

1 Shakespear, J, The Thirty Forth Division p.102.

2 Ewing, J. The Royal Scots 1914-1919 (Oliver & Boyd 1925) p.396.

3 Simpson, C.R. (Ed) The History of the Lincolnshire Regiment 1914-1918 (Medici Society 1931) p.225.

4 Ternan, T. The Story of the Tyneside Scottish (Newcastle c.1919) p.156-157.

5 Falls, C. Military Operations France and Belgium 1917 Volume 1 (HMSO 1940) p.233.

6 Quoted in Shakespear op cit. p.101.

7 London Gazette 8th June 1917 PRO ZJ1.

8 For further information see Gliddon, G. VCs of the First World War: Arras & Messines 1917 (Alan Sutton 1998).

9 Shakespear op cit. p.105-106.

10 London Gazette 8th June 1917 PRO ZJ1.

11 Falls op cit p.235.

12 Bewsher, F.W. The History of the Fifty First (Highland) Division 1914-1918 (1920) p.155.

13 At Cambrai in November 1917, Harper's Division failed to capture the Flesquieres Ridge, partly because of a refusal to adopt the suggested pattern of infantry-tank co-operation. It makes interesting speculation as to how the outcome of this battle might have been different if Harper's earlier experience with the tanks had been more positive.

14 Bewsher op cit. p.155-156.

15 ibid. p.156.

16 Captain A.T. Saulez, D/64 RFA, was killed on 22nd April 1917 and is buried in Bailleul Road East Cemetery.

17 Bewsher op cit. p.158.

18 For more information on this see an article on the subject on the author's website, The Old Front Line.

Chapter 3

XVII CORPS: 4TH AND 9TH (SCOTTISH) DIVISIONS
9th/10th APRIL 1917

The Battle

XVII Corps, commanded by Lieutenant General Sir Charles Fergusson, constituted the northern sector of British forces at Arras on 9th April 1917; beyond them were the Canadian Corps assaulting Vimy Ridge. XVII Corps consisted of four divisions, with 34th and 51st (Highland) Division on the left flank attacking what was effectively the southern extension of Vimy Ridge; and 4th and 9th (Scottish) Divisions on the right, advancing across the area north of the River Scarpe. It is this latter fighting which will be dealt with here; the other formations are covered elsewhere in the book.

Order of Battle for the advance near St Laurent, 9th April 1917.

Veterans of Arras – two soldiers of the Royal Scots who fought with the 9th (Scottish) Division, 1917.

There were several differences with this part of the advance compared to elsewhere on the battlefield on 9th April. The 9th (Scottish) Division (Major General H.T.Lukin) had one of the widest fronts that day, with all three brigades in the line. Behind it was the 4th Division and here, instead of one Brigade leap-frogging another, it would be a case of an entire division passing through to continue with the push. 9th Division had a fine fighting tradition, being the first New Army formation and veteran of the Battle of Loos and the Somme. Due to losses at Loos, one brigade had been disbanded and replaced with the South African Brigade, who had distinguished themselves at Delville Wood in July 1916. Their original commander was now leading the Division; this was Lukin's first big battle since his promotion the previous December.

The division had four tanks from No 7 Company, C Battalion Heavy Branch Machine Gun Corps attached to them, and a clever barrage to protect the men as they moved forward. The Commander Royal Artillery (CRA), Brigadier General H.H.Tudor (who would rise to command the division in 1918), had mixed one in four rounds with smoke and there were sufficient guns to ensure the smoke screen would be thick enough. This was not normal practice and Allenby's Third Army instructions had dictated that half the shells contained High Explosive, half shrapnel but, it was later recorded,

> ... it appears that the artillery orders of the 9th Division were not submitted to higher authority in detail for fear that a categorical order to conform to this instruction would be the result.[1]

This was clear thinking by the CRA; the men of his Division were to advance over open ground, across a considerable distance, and through terrain cut by long valleys. In the latter it would be difficult to estimate angles of sight, and Tudor feared the shrapnel would be ineffective under such conditions. These changing tactics, which originated from the Somme, were part of a more general learning curve in the entire army and such ideas would be more commonplace as the war progressed.

Lukin's division had three objectives. The 26th and 27th Brigades of Scottish troops would capture the initial German positions on the Black Line, then go forward to the Blue Line, which rested on the Arras-Lens railway line. At this point it was in a cutting and flanked by two trenches. From here the South African Brigade would pass through and capture the Brown Line with some elements of 27th Brigade. Here their left flank would rest on the Douai road at Point du Jour, meeting up with 34th Division on the left, and the right flank would extend to include the village of Athies. At this point the division would go no further, awaiting the arrival of 4th Division to carry the advance to the last objective, the Green Line beyond Fampoux. It was an ambitious plan and, if successful, would see the greatest advance of any British formation since the deadlock of trench warfare began.

At Zero Hour Tudor's barrage intensified.

At 5.30am our guns opened with a deafening crash. Overhead the rushing steel sounded like a frenzied discord combining the deep boom of the drum with the shrill shriek of the whistle, and where the shells landed, the earth leaped up in a mad barbaric dance. A gigantic wall of smoke and fire lay right along the enemy's line, and sprays of coloured lights, shooting up from his trenches, betokened the anxiety and distress of the garrison.[2]

The advance to the Black Line went well. Aside from a few smoke shells dropping short on the 6th KOSB as they waited to move forward, the objective was reached in time. 7th Seaforth Highlanders stormed the village of St Laurent and took the 'Island' just north of Blangy, where 15th (Scottish) were attacking on the right. As 8th Black Watch reached Wish Trench, they captured the regimental commander of 8th Bavarians, along with his adjutant. Confused by the barrage, neither had seemingly realised a battle was in progress. To the north, 12th Royal Scots were the right-hand battalion of 27th Brigade. Their advance started in No Man's Land.

Our troops, mustered in mine craters fringing the front line trenches... swarmed into No Man's Land, fanning out into the formations in which they were to carry out the attack. With the first lift of the barrage the entire line swept forward, and the only difficulty experienced by our troops was in recognising the hostile trenches, which had been so completely flattened by our barrage that in many places they were scarcely distinguishable from the cavernous holes scooped by our heavy shells... The men pressed forward with such ardour that they ran into our barrage, and while 200 yards from Obermayer Trench (the first objective) Lieutenant Colonel Thorne was killed, probably by one of our own shells.[3]

Thorne had only commanded the battalion for just over a month, having come to the Royal Scots from the 4th Royal Berkshire Regiment.[4]

As the Black Line was passed, the men detailed to 'mop-up' the trenches came on. However, due to the powerful bombardment, many had problems recognising exactly where the German positions had been. This meant that in some cases groups of Germans were overlooked, but not always. In a sunken lane just beyond Obermayer Trench, 6th KOSB found '...swarms of the 25th Bavarians crouching in the dug-outs'.[5] But on the front of 27th Brigade, a lone German machine-gun had been overlooked. Its crew emerged with the weapon and laid down heavy fire into the rear of 9th Seaforths, the Division's pioneer battalion;

> *... the men dropped their shovels, picked up their rifles and after killing its crew, carried off the machine-gun as a trophy.[6]*

The assault on the Blue Line began at 7.36am. This strong position along the Arras-Lens railway line had worried Lukin, but the

The ruins of St Laurent, taken by the 9th (Scottish) Division.

bombardment had done its job. The only major problems were close to the Railway Triangle, where elements of 26th Brigade were held up until troops from 15th (Scottish) Division and their tank finally cleared it. The South African Brigade had also come into action now, and while some of its men in the 3rd and 4th Battalions had problems clearing the wire that screened the railway cutting, they were protected by a further smoke screen laid by the 13-pounder field guns of 'F' Battery Royal Horse Artillery. As they entered the cutting, the South Africans accounted for all the machine-guns and, '... of the garrison on the Railway not one escaped; all were killed or captured'.[7]

The Blue Line was now secure, and there were a few changes in disposition to allow the next troops to leap-frog and continue to the Brown Line, the final objective as far as 9th Division was concerned. The tanks assisting the Division, four of them, had all failed to make it beyond the Blue Line, the final one ditching 200 yards short of the railway cutting. Meanwhile, the 5th Cameron Highlanders and 10th Argylls from 26th Brigade, 11th Royal Scots from 27th, and 1st and 2nd Battalions SAI from South African Brigade, passed through and arrived on the Blue Line. Here they would all wait for the next phase, which eventually proved a delay of four hours. In the interim, a German spotter plane came over and directed fire onto the railway cutting, but thankfully few men were crowding there and casualties were few.

At 12.16pm these five battalions started the next attack. On the whole '... the assault on the Brown Line took the form of an orderly procession',[8] but in the north around Point du Jour 11th Royal Scots encountered uncut wire.

> With such an obstacle in front of them, even a few men could have held up a Division. But the enemy had been stupefied by the swiftness of out advance and the loss of his strong forward entrenchments, and made no serious attempt to stem the rush of the Royal Scots. While the Jocks were laboriously threading their way through the maze of uncut wire, they could see in the distance scores of Germans bolting in panic-stricken terror to the east.[9]

Brigadier General Lawson, commanding the South Africans, later reported some uncut wire on his front as well, but the 1st and 2nd SAI took their objectives in the junction of Oynx and Paint trenches with only just over thirty fatal casualties.[10] With all objectives now reached and held, 9th Division handed over to 4th Division for the next stage of the battle.

The German trench system near St Laurent.

Major General the Hon. W. Lambton's 4th Division had been in France since August 1914, and had fought in almost every engagement since. Few of the original regulars were left by 1917, but a handful were still there, often in senior positions commanding companies and battalions. Lambton himself had commanded the formation since September 1915, and seen his men through some trying times on the Somme in 1916. Just prior to Arras there had been some reorganisation of personnel in the formation, as described by Brigadier General Adrian Carton de Wiart VC.

The 4th Division was commanded by General Billy

Advance of the 4th Division on Fampoux, 9th April 1917.

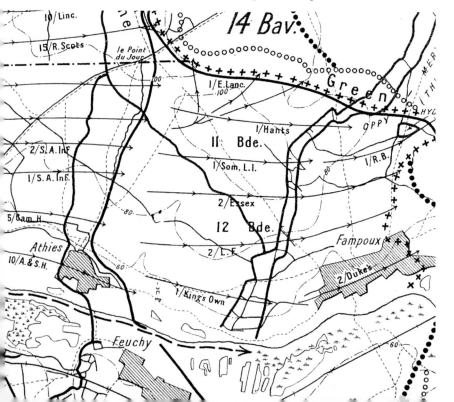

The men of 12th Company MGC on the eve of the Battle of Arras.

Lambton, a charming man, though unapproachable in the early morning! This division had had a hard time; it had lost its spirit and gone stale with weariness, and General Lambton was given a new set of brigade commanders to pull it together.[11]

On the eve of the battle the whole Division had been billeted at Maroeuil, north-west of Arras, and had come up through the suburb of St Catherine in sleet and snow to its assembly area at St Nicholas, close to the front line. Here the men were given a warm meal, which was welcome in the awful weather conditions, before moving up. As they progressed, Carton de Wiart noticed some work by the Engineers at the side of the road.

… where some bright staff officer in a rush of zeal had chosen to have a trench dug adorned with a large notice, 'Reserved for the English dead'. I hoped it was not ominous![12]

The Blue Line was reached by midday and, as it approached the Brown Line, Brigadier General Carton de Wiart VC's 12th Brigade came under shell fire, suffering some losses. De Wiart himself was already wounded, having been hit the day before, but characteristically stayed

81

The Athies road and the Scarpe valley.

at his post with his men. At 3.15pm the final assault went in. To the south 2nd Essex, 2nd Lancashire Fusiliers and 1st King's Own of 12th Brigade crossed the Oppy-Mericourt Line of defences after being met by some '…wild rifle fire'[13], while 2nd Duke of Wellington's came through at 4.40pm and captured the village of Fampoux. In this it was protected by a special howitzer barrage, moving ahead at the rate of 100 yards in four minutes. House to house fighting followed amid the rubble of the village, despite the fact that a shell from a 15-inch gun from Corps artillery had ignited an ammunition dump causing much damage. However, progress beyond the village was impossible, as machine-gun fire from the railway line to the south stopped 12th Brigade 500 yards short of the Green Line. Carton de Wiart went up to have a look with one of his staff officers, but realised that for now they would have to stay where they were.

To the north 11th Brigade entered the Oppy-Mericourt Line spearheaded by 1st Somerset Light Infantry and 1st Hampshires. The Somersets encountered a lot more uncut wire, but in most places managed to find the defenders' own access gaps and effected an entry;

> … for a moment there was hesitation, then several tracks through the German wire were found and along these the men rushed towards the enemy's trenches. Others… climbed the wire,

whilst their comrades halted and shot down any Germans who showed themselves about the parapets... The cool manner in which some of the Somerset men thus covered the advance... was too much for the shattered Germans, the majority of whom put up their hands and surrendered.[14]

1st Hampshires had similar problems with the wire, but by 4pm they had secured their section of the Oppy-Mericourt Line, taking eighty prisoners and capturing three German howitzers. The casualties for such an attack were considered 'trifling'; one officer died of wounds, two others and six other ranks were wounded.

1st Rifle Brigade passed through; its objective to take Hyderabad Redoubt on the Fampoux-Gavrelle road. One officer of the Battalion later recalled;

Soon after getting through the fourth system we came under machine-gun fire from an inn on the Roeux-Gavrelle road and from Gavrelle. We soon managed to pick out the redoubt on account of the masses of wire which surrounded it, which we could see was completely intact. On our way up to it a large black dog came galloping along to meet us. When we came within twenty yards of it a football was drop-kicked by Corporal Bancroft into the redoubt and the place was rushed. The various mopping up parties... started clearing the dug-outs and after a time seven officers and nine men appeared. A staff officer tried to bolt down the road to Gavrelle and was at once shot by C Company's sniping corporal.[15]

Parties from the same Battalion captured a German general in the sunken lane south of the redoubt, who had come up to observe. He had arranged to have his car close by, but his driver had deserted him and the officer was taken prisoner.

For now the advance was going no further, but the way ahead to Roeux and Gavrelle had been opened. During the night of 9th/10th April a German counter-attack took place, with groups of infantry moving up in artillery formation, but this was dispersed by machine-gun fire and a protective barrage and was not pressed home. The men of 4th and 9th Division no doubt felt some pride in their achievement as the day came to a close. Indeed, this operation,

... marked the longest advance made that day and the longest made in a single day by any belligerent on the Western Front since trench warfare had set in; it was a distance of 3½ miles.[16]

Spider Corner – the railway bridge that led the way to Battery Valley.

<u>A Walk in the 4th & 9th Divisional Sectors</u>

This walk takes about 3½ hours and covers the main areas where 4th and 9th (Scottish) Divisions fought in the opening phase of the advance. It is a circular walk, starting and ending at Athies Communal Cemetery. Cemeteries referred to in bold are described in detail below.

Park your car close to **Athies Communal Cemetery Extension**. There is some parking in a small housing development alongside the cemetery: in Rue des Bouvreuils, for example. Having visited the cemetery, join the D37 and go right, uphill. On reaching a crest there are good views west, back towards Arras and St Laurant Blangy, where the front lines were on the morning of 9th April 1917. This was the location of the Blue and the Black Line objectives, but today much of the ground has been swallowed up in building development and new roads.

Stay on the D37 until it meets the main N50 Arras-Douai road. This

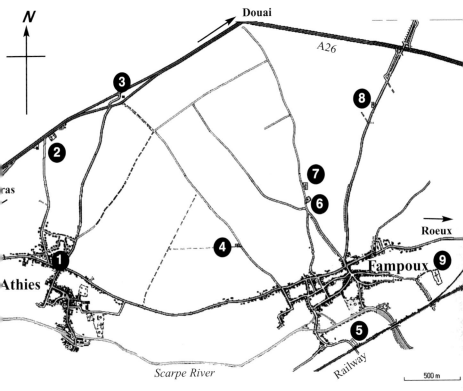

1. Arties Communal Cemetery Extensions
2. Point du Jour Cemetery
3. 9th Division Memorial
4. Fampoux British Cemetery
5. Level Crossing Cemetery
6. Seaforths Memorial
7. Sunken Road Cemetery
8. Chili Trench Cemetery
9. Brown's Copse Cemetery

is a very fast road, and extreme care should be taken to cross it to reach the memorial cairn to the 9th (Scottish) Division on the Point du Jour. This memorial was built in the 1920s, using stone brought specially from the areas of Scotland where the Division drew its original enlistments in September 1914. The advance at Arras was one of its greatest wartime achievements,

The memorial to 9th (Scottish) Division on the Point du Jour. It seems that it is planned to move this memorial.

recognised by the award of the Distinguished Conduct Medal to the Division, and this was the obvious place to erect a divisional memorial. A small section of trench in a piece of pock-marked ground is all that remains of the Brown Line objective, taken by men of 6th KOSB on 9th April. The names of the units that served with the Division during the war are on stones by the road, and the battle honours listed on the main memorial.

Re-cross the N50 (again taking extreme care), and take a track that parallels this road. Then follow it right, as it cross the fields in the direction of Fampoux. At the next cross-roads of tracks go straight across, and follow it gradually downhill. You are now coming into the area fought over by elements of 4th Division, after they had leap-frogged through 9th (Scottish) Division following the capture of the Brown Line objective. Stay on this track until you reach the secluded, and rarely visited **Fampoux British Cemetery**.

Leave the cemetery and turn right, continuing along the track to where it meets the main D42 road. Here turn left and follow into Fampoux village. This is ground captured by 1st King's Own and 2nd Duke of Wellingtons on 9th April, fought from house to house in the ruins of the village. The walk could be extended at this point by taking the next road on the right, and following the green CWGC signs to **Level Crossing Cemetery** in Fampoux, which is about 500 metres away. If you do visit this cemetery, retrace your steps afterwards. Otherwise visit this cemetery by car later and continue on the D42 to the church in central Fampoux and turn left. You will pass the communal cemetery, where there are war graves from the Second World War.

Stay on this track until you reach a junction; go straight across and just on the right is the memorial to 2nd Seaforth Highlanders. This unit from 4th Division made an attack from this sunken lane on 11th April 1917 with 1st Royal Irish Fusiliers, which was costly for both battalions (this is described in greater detail in Chapter 9 about Roeux). Leaving the memorial, continue along this minor road to the Sunken Road Cemetery. There are good views here across to the site of the Hyderabad Redoubt.

Leaving the cemetery, turn right and stay on the minor road. There are good views further along towards Gavrelle, where the Royal Naval Division fought in April 1917.[17] Take the second minor road on the left, a little short of the motorway, and follow this as it runs parallel to this road until you reach a junction of tracks. Here go straight across, and follow this downhill until it meets the D37. Here turn left, and continue to Athies Communal Cemetery Extension and your vehicle.

Associated Cemeteries

ATHIES COMMUNAL CEMETERY EXTENSION:
There is one war grave among the civilian graves in the Communal Cemetery: a soldier of the Royal Army Medical Corps who was killed attached to the South African Medical Corps on 12th April 1917. The main burials are in the extension.

The cemetery was started after the capture of the village, and was used by Field Ambulances (which had an ADS located in Athies) and front line units until May 1918, and then again in September 1918. Burials total: 286 British, twenty-one South African, one Australian, and one German. There are thirty-two unknowns, only about ten per cent (low for an Arras cemetery) and three Special Memorials.

Following the capture of Athies, the area was used extensively by divisional Royal Field Artillery (RFA) gun batteries who had their gun-sites nearby. Graves in the cemetery reflect this, with a large proportion being gunners. Among them was Major W.H. Smith (B-9), A/52 RFA, who was killed in action on 12th April 1917. He was educated at St. Faith's School, Cambridge, Blundell's School, Tiverton and Sidney Sussex College, Cambridge. Smith was also an artist, and a student of the Royal Academy, London, and the Slade School of Art. An Australian gunner is also found here: Gunner E.E. Woodland (E-26) of the 36th Australian Heavy Artillery Group was in a unit equipped with 9.2-inch howitzers. He was killed on 30th April 1917, aged only twenty. By this time his unit had moved up to Athies and was firing on the German positions at the Roeux chemical works and beyond.

J.P. Ellis (H-6) was Regimental Sergeant Major of 1st Bn Royal Irish Fusiliers. A regular soldier from Slingsby in Yorkshire, who had previous service with the Grenadier Guards, he was killed on 11th April 1917. On this day his Battalion launched an ill-fated and costly attacked on Roeux, alongside the 2nd Seaforth Highlanders. This attack will be discussed in more detail in the chapter on Roeux. Cavalry played more of a part in the Battle of Arras than is widely known and a number of cavalry graves are found in this cemetery, among them Corporal of Horse C.T. Ruddle (H-3), of the Household Battalion, who was killed near Fampoux on 11th April 1917.

FAMPOUX BRITISH CEMETERY
Fampoux was captured by the 4th Division (having leap-frogged through the 9th (Scottish) Division) on 9th April 1917). It remained close behind the British front line for the rest of the battle, and some

ground was lost in the German offensive on 25th March 1918 until it was retaken by the 51st (Highland) Division on 26th August 1918. Fampoux British Cemetery (called at one time Helena Trench Cemetery) was made by the units of 4th and 34th Divisions in April-June 1917 and used again by the Guards Division in 1918. After the Armistice it was found necessary to regroup ten graves (now forming Row E), which projected into the road, and the numbering of Rows A to D is therefore irregular. Burials total ninety-nine British and nineteen South African graves.

The cemetery contains a good mix of men from 4th and 9th (Scottish) Divisions, especially 2nd Essex from the former and South Africans from the latter. Among some of the later graves is Lieutenant A.L.G. Hider (A-46) of 8th South Staffs who died on 27th May 1917, aged twenty-three. He was 'an old Westminster City school boy'. Captain F.C. Napier (B-10) of 1st Kings Own had taken part in the advance on Fampoux on 9th April, only to be killed just beyond it on 3rd May 1917, aged forty-three.

HERVIN FARM BRITISH CEMETERY

Until the 9th April 1917 the British front line ran practically through the nearby village of St Laurent Blangy. Hervin Farm British Cemetery is south of the road from St. Laurent-Blangy to Fampoux, a little east of the railway embankment. Hervin Farm, which was taken by the units of the 9th (Scottish) Division on 9th April 1917, is on the other side of the railway. The cemetery was made by fighting units and Field Ambulances from April 1917, and three graves were added subsequently. It contains the graves of fifty-one British soldiers, of whom three are unidentified.

Two senior officers are buried in Hervin Farm. Lieutenant Colonel S.G. Mullock, Essex Regiment, was killed on 12th April 1917. Brigadier General C. Gosling CMG, was a King's Royal Rifle Corps officer, commanding 10th Brigade of 4th Division. Gosling had been first commissioned in 1888, and commanded 3rd KRRC in France from 1914, being badly wounded at St Eloi in February 1915. Appointed to command 7th Brigade of 25th Division, he had been wounded again near Vimy Ridge in May 1916. He was also killed on 12th April 1917, by shell fire. His Brigade Major, Captain H.G.A. Fellowes MC, of the 11th Lancers, was killed by a sniper and is buried alongside him.

Hervin Farm Cemetery.

Grave of Brig-Gen C.Gosling
CMG, commanding 10th
Brigade.

Brig-Gen Charles Gosling CMG.

Level Crossing Cemetery.

LEVEL CROSSING CEMETERY, FAMPOUX

Taken on the first day of the Battle of Arras, Fampoux remained behind the British lines until March 1918 when part of the village was captured by the Germans. It was finally retaken by the 51st (Highland) Division on 26th August 1918. The cemetery was started in June 1917, when a number of isolated graves from April and May were brought in from the surrounding battlefield, and remained in use until March 1918; two further burials were made in October 1918. The 15th (Scottish) Division, as well as the 9th and 51st Division, fought in the area, and over half the graves are those of soldiers of Scottish regiments – giving it very much a Scottish 'feel'. Burials total: 400 British, two South African, thirty unknown and one Special Memorial.

The officers of 7th Argyll and Sutherland Highlanders are well represented in Plot I, Row A. Four of them killed in the fighting at Roeux are buried here. Lieutenant Colonel U.L. Hooke (I-C-35), was killed commanding 3/4th Queens on 21st June 1917, aged thirty-six. Casualties from the Guards Division, who served here during the winter of 1917/18, are noticeable in Plot II. Among them is an elderly subaltern, Second Lieutenant C.E. Penfold Ballard (II-B-14), 1st Welsh Guards, who was killed on 10th March 1918, aged forty-nine.

POINT DU JOUR CEMETERY

Athies was captured by the 9th (Scottish) Division, which included the South African Brigade, on 9th April 1917 and afterwards it remained in British hands for the rest of the war. Point du Jour was, in times of peace, a house on the road from St. Laurent-Blangy to Gavrelle; in 1917 it was a German redoubt in the Brown Line, captured by elements of the 34th Division on 9th April. Two cemeteries were made on the right of the road from St. Laurent-Blangy to Point du Jour, and that which was called No. 1 is the present Point du Jour Military Cemetery. It was used from April to November 1917, and again in May 1918. At the time of the Armistice it contained eighty-two graves (now part of Plot I). It was then enlarged by the concentration of graves from the battlefields and small cemeteries north, east and south of Arras. Burials total: 627 British, sixty-eight South African, twenty four Royal Guernsey Light Infantry, fourteen Canadian, two New Zealand and three French. There are also a small number of Second World War casualties buried here, largely from May 1940. Of the First World War graves, nearly half are unidentified and Special Memorials are erected to sixteen British soldiers and six from South Africa. Other special memorials record the names of six British soldiers, buried in other cemeteries, whose graves were destroyed by shell fire. The bodies of forty-four unidentified French soldiers have been removed to another cemetery. In April 2002 the bodies of a number of unknown soldiers of the Lincolnshire Regiment and Royal Naval Division, found near the Point du Jour, were reburied here.

The following cemeteries were among those concentrated into Point du Jour:

BROWN LINE CEMETERY, ST. LAURENT-BLANGY: some 800 metres north of that village, it was named from one of the objectives on the 9th April 1917. The cemetery contained the graves of thirty-two soldiers from South Africa and one from the United Kingdom, who died on that day.

EFFIE TRENCH CEMETERY, ATHIES: was 460 metres South of the Point-du-Jour. It contained the graves of twenty-two soldiers of the 1st East Lancs and the Royal Field Artillery, who died in April and May 1917.

EVIN-MALMAISON COMMUNAL CEMETERY: contained the graves of six soldiers from the United Kingdom and one from Canada, buried by the enemy in 1917; one of these graves was not removed.

HENIN-LIETARD COMMUNAL CEMETERY: contained the graves of thirteen soldiers of the 12th (Eastern) Division, which occupied Henin-Lietard on 12th October 1918.

LONELY HOUSE CEMETERY, GAVRELLE: located between the Point-du-Jour and Gavrelle, contained the graves of twenty-five sailors, soldiers and Marines from the United Kingdom, who fell in April-July 1917.

POINT-DU-JOUR MILITARY CEMETERY No 2: which was very close to the present cemetery, contained the graves of fifteen soldiers from the United Kingdom who fell in April-June 1917.

QUARRY CEMETERY, FAMPOUX: at the West end of Fampoux village, contained the graves of twenty-five soldiers from the United Kingdom and eight from South Africa, who fell between 11th and 12th April 1917.

SUNKEN ROAD CEMETERY, FAMPOUX
Fampoux was taken by the 4th Division on the 9th April 1917, lost at the end of March 1918 and retaken at the end of the following August. Sunken Road Cemetery is at the summit of the sunken road to Bailleul, on the east side. It was made by Burial Officers and fighting units in the period between April 1917 and January 1918. It contains the graves of 196 British soldiers, of whom twenty-six are unidentified; but sixteen of these graves, destroyed by shell fire, are now represented by Special Memorials.

1 Falls, C. Military Operations France and Belgium 1917 Volume 1 (HMSO 1940) p.227.
2 Ewing, J. The History of the 9th (Scottish) Division 1914-1919 (John Murray 1921) p.193-194.
3 Ewing, J. The Royal Scots 1914-1919 (Oliver & Boyd 1925) p.391-392.
4 Lt-Col H.U.H.Thorne, KIA 9.4.17. Buried St Nicholas British Cemetery.
5 Ewing The History of the 9th (Scottish) Division 1914-1919 op cit. p.195.
6 ibid.
7 ibid. p.196.
8 ibid. p.197.
9 Ewing The Royal Scots 1914-1919 op cit. p.394
10 See Digby, P.K.A. Pyramids & Poppies: The 1st SA Infantry Brigade in Libya, France and Flanders 1915-1919 (Ashanti Publishing 1993) p.197-207.
11 Carton de Wiart, A. Happy Odyssey (Jonathon Cape 1950) p.79-80.
12 ibid. p.81.
13 Falls op cit. p.230.
14 Wyrall, E. The History of the Somerset Light Infantry 1914-1919 (Methuen & Co Ltd 1927) p.173-174.
15 Seymour, W. The History of the Rifle Brigade in the War of 1914-1918 Vol II (Rifle brigade Club 1936) p.30.
16 Falls op cit. p.231.
17 See Tallet, K. & Tasker, T. Arras – Gavrelle (Pen & Sword 1999).

Chapter 4

VI CORPS: 3RD, 12TH (EASTERN) AND 15TH (SCOTTISH) DIVISIONS

9th/10th APRIL 1917

The Battle

VI Corps was commanded by Lieutenant General J.A.L. Haldane and for the advance on 9th April comprised 3rd, 12th (Eastern) and 15th (Scottish) Divisions. The 37th Division were in reserve beyond Arras and available to be committed if the advance went well. The Corps line of attack went from Tilloy les Mofflaines in the south, where it bordered on VII Corps, and the Scarpe River around Blangy. These were positions that dated back to 1914, and aside from a few hundred yards of trench near Tilloy, the situation on the Corps' front had not changed during the German withdrawal to the Hindenburg Line. As such the infrastructure on the British side was firmly in place, with light railways, canal barges to the suburbs of Arras and a whole system of tunnels, passageways and subterranean caverns in which to shelter troops. VI Corps objectives involved the capture of the forward

The advance of VI Corps on 9th April 1917.

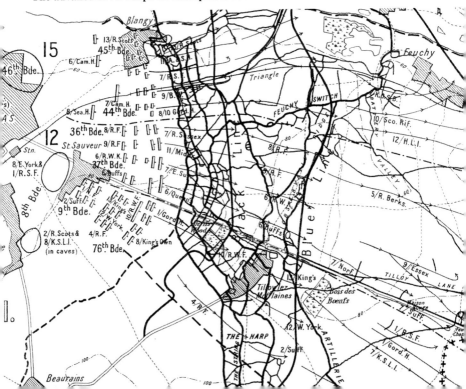

The view from the German front line towards Arras.

positions, or the Black Line, then advancing to the Blue Line, which was a northern extension of the *Artillerie Schutzstellung* that ended near Battery Valley. From here they would push on the main objective, the Wancourt-Feuchy line, and thus link up with elements of VII Corps on the right. This would open the way for 37th Division to come up and take Monchy le Preux – the prize on the high ground beyond.

Artillery support came in the form of nine groups of 6-inch howitzer units, with five of 8-inch and six 9.2-inch. In addition there were six 60-pounder batteries, six 6-inch guns, a 9.2-inch on a railway mounting and one mammoth 15-inch which fired shells that weighed more than a ton each. This was aside from the divisional artillery, which was largely allocated wire cutting and targets around the Black Line. Tank support was also available, with two pairs of Mk IIs from

Assault troops move up for the attack on Tilloy.

No 9 company allocated to 3rd Division at Tilloy, some from No 8 closer to the Harp, two on 12th Division front and two detailed to attack the Railway Triangle defences on 15th Division's line of advance.

The 3rd Division (Major General C.J. Deverell) in the south were to attack from the British trenches at St Sauveur towards Tilloy les Mofflaines. Their frontage was narrow near the village, only about half a mile, but as their advance continued eastwards it would expand to nearly a mile as they reached the Wancourt-Feuchy line. On the right the German positions were affected by the withdrawal and it was known that the forward posts were only lightly manned, if at all. At Zero Hour, 5.30am, the leading battalion, 1st Gordon Highlanders, went in under cover of a hurricane bombardment of Stokes mortars and indirect machine-gun fire. Here it reached and captured the German fourth line, while 10th Royal Welsh Fusiliers came up and took Devil's Wood on the Black Line. Both were achieved with few losses. 9th Brigade, which had been sheltering safe in the caves at Ronville, then came through St Sauveur and passed the Black Line at 7.30am. The spearhead of this attack was 4th Royal Fusiliers, who were to take the String and the sunken road to the east, and 2nd Suffolks (from 76th Brigade) whose objective was the Harp itself. On their left flank were 12th West Yorks and 13th King's Liverpools who were to head for the Bois des Boeufs.

4th Royal Fusiliers came under heavy shell fire as they crossed the open. Ahead of them Telegraph Hill dominated the landscape, looking down at them as they crossed a mile of ground before reaching the German lines. Despite casualties, they managed to keep formation and moved in on the String. Casualties mounted from rifle and machine gun fire, one company losing all its officers. The first man into the objective was Second Lieutenant the Earl of Shannon[1], who had led his men in despite being wounded.[1] The regimental historian noted that,

> ... before this trench, with its wire only partially cut, many losses were sustained. A portion of the company carried on with the 9th Rifle Brigade to Neuilly Trench. Z Company were caught by the fire from the north-east corner of Tilloy village, but with the help of two platoons... assisted in the capture of Lynx and String trenches... The battalion gained little support from the tanks, although one sat down upon Nomeny Trench after they had carried it. Among the captures of the day were 5 officers and 70 other ranks, three machine-guns, two Minnenwerfer and four Granatenwerfer.[2]

The ruins of Tilloy les Moifflaines, close to the chateau.

However, losses in 4th Royal Fusiliers amounted to 225 officers and men.

On the left 13th King's were held up in the Bois de Boeufs and the grounds of the chateau which adjoined it. This was largely due to the failure of the tank support; most of the tanks allocated to the Division had stuck in the mud en-route to the front line, and the supply trucks which serviced them could not get up to assist, delayed by conditions in Arras itself. Eventually the position was secured, giving 8th Brigade its chance to leap through and continue to the Wancourt-Feuchy line.

8th Brigade passed through around noon on 9th April, with 2nd Royal Scots and 7th KSLI in the lead. Their advance was roughly parallel with the Cambrai road on their left and, although they came under sniper fire from the few survivors of the German garrison in Tilloy, they soon swept over several lines of trenches taking a number of prisoners. From here the units moved towards the Wancourt-Feuchy line, but

> *... our artillery barrage was less sustained and less accurate than it was in the first stages of the battle, and as the 8th Brigade*

The main street in Tilloy.

swept on its ranks were raked by fire from a strong-point known as Church Work near Feuchy Chapel. By the time Chapel Road was reached, this fire was so intense that the left of the brigade could make no progress. The Royal Scots, veering to the south, managed to push forward some distance and seized another hostile trench, but at this point they were subjected to terrific machine-gun fire from the south as well as the north. It was suicidal to continue the advance.[3]

However, a further attempt to reach the final objective was made in the late afternoon, when 1st Gordon Highlanders and 8th King's Own were ordered up. These orders arrived late at the King's Own, and they were therefore behind from the start. The Gordons therefore went in on their own, but were forced back on the slopes of Chapel Hill by the same machine-gun fire. Until the Chapel Work, on the front of 12th (Eastern) Division, could be cleared, success was impossible.

Major General Arthur B. Scott's 12th (Eastern) Division was one of those that had a high reputation. It was a veteran formation of Loos and the Somme, and was very much an Arras division; having been on this front in mid-1916, and again from late that year until the battle. Scott had been in command since October 1915, and

> *.. won the esteem and regard of all ranks by his constant courtesy and kindness, as well as the admiration of all for his leadership and soldierly character.[4]*

It held a front from the Arras-Cambrai road in the south to the boundary with 15th (Scottish) Division, just south of Blangy. The troops in the two attacking brigades, 36th and 37th, had fully utilised the system of tunnels, caves and subways below Arras prior to the battle. Consequently they suffered no casualties prior to Zero Hour and

Forward observers from the 12th (Eastern) Division in action near Tilloy.

were fully rested. Deep dugouts in the front line further sheltered the men and some of the subways were extended on the eve of the advance so that exits went out into No Man's Land. One officer wrote,

> ... *now it is possible to get from the crypt of the Cathedral* [in Arras] *to under the German wire without braving one shell in the open.*[5]

The plan for this Division was to advance to the Black Line with the two spearhead Brigades, then the 35th in reserve would pass through them and take the Brown Line – the northern extension of the Wancourt-Feuchy line. The ground ahead of them rose to a high point on Observation Hill, with Orange Hill beyond that. The Germans therefore had the advantage of looking down on any attack. To make up for this a large smoke bombardment was planned to screen the advance, largely from the gun sites in Battery Valley which were only 2,500 yards from the British front line.

At Zero Hour the 37th Brigade attacked on the right, covered by a machine-gun barrage from twenty-four Vickers machine-guns. Using these weapons like artillery was now becoming more and more commonplace. The 6th Queen's and 7th East Surreys were leading just north of the main road. 36th Brigade comprising, in the initial wave, 7th Royal Sussex and 11th Middlesex, who were on the left. They soon reached the Black Line and the experience of the Royal Sussex was common to them all.

> *It was then that the full effect of the preliminary bombardment was realised, for little, if anything, remained of the enemy wire and trenches. In the darkness and smoke it was extremely difficult to find our way, and the ground bore no resemblance to the neat trenches over which we had practised so carefully at Lignereuil. We met with very little opposition from the dazed enemy and gained all the objectives up to time. A and B companies entered the front line trench together and, finding little resistance, went on to the fourth line.*[6]

The other units of the two brigades then passed through, en-route to the Blue Line. This attack saw the 8th and 9th Royal Fusiliers on the left, with 6th Royal West Kents and 6th Buffs on the right. An 'egg-shaped' redoubt (known as Houlette Work on British maps, and Lemburg-Shanze to the Germans) just north of Tilloy proved especially troublesome in this phase of operations, until cleared by rifle grenades from 6th Buffs.

> *After some stiff hand-to-hand fighting, D Company was able to get round to the flank and, by overcoming concealed machine-*

Artillery moves up through the Arras cemetery.

> *guns, which the enemy had pushed forward into shell holes, reached and captured the point on the Blue Line which was its objective.... Great numbers of prisoners, machine guns, field guns and materiel fell to the Buffs.*[7]

Casualties for the advance were two officers and twenty-three men killed, seven officers and 149 men wounded, with eighteen missing.

The 8th and 9th Royal Fusiliers coming up on the left also advanced to their objectives. In the 8th Battalion the men moved off their front line so quickly that they mingled with the 7th Royal Sussex, reaching the German positions without a single loss. Two strong points en-route to the Blue Line were outflanked, this final objective being reached by 10am with minimal casualties. Whilst consolidating a large number of prisoners were taken, some of them herded in deep dugouts. It was soon realised these structures could be dangerous:

> *... the dugouts were unhealthy places. One of them, in the 11th Middlesex area, was suddenly blown up by the explosion of a mine; and as a consequence German dug-outs were afterwards forbidden.*[8]

During the consolidation in the Blue Line, the 7th East Surreys came under fire. They had already suffered heavy losses among the officers, with four killed and two wounded. In the midst of these problems platoon sergeants took over, one of whom was Sergeant Harry Cator MM. Cator was born at Drayton, Norwich, in 1894, and worked as a railway porter near Thakenham. For some reason he joined the 7th East Surreys, and served in France with them from 1915. Like many soldiers who fought at Arras, Cator was a veteran of the Somme, where he had been awarded the Military Medal for bravery at Ovillers. In the advance on 9th April, he went out with a comrade and took on the defenders of Hangest Trench on his own. For this he was eventually awarded the Victoria Cross. His citation reads:

For most conspicuous bravery and devotion to duty. Whilst consolidating the first-line captured system his platoon suffered severe casualties from hostile machine-gun and rifle fire. In full view of the enemy and under heavy fire, Sgt Cator with one man advanced across the open to attack the hostile machine-gun. The man accompanying him was killed after going a short distance, but Sgt Cator continued on, and picking up a Lewis gun and some drums on his way, succeeded in reaching the northern end of the hostile trench. Meanwhile one of our bombing parties were seen to be held up by a machine-gun. Sgt Cator took up a position from which he sighted this gun, and killed the entire team and the officer, whose papers he brought in. He continued to hold that end of the trench with the Lewis gun with such effect that the bombing squad was enabled to work along, the result being that 100 prisoners and five machine-guns were captured.[9]

Sergeant Harry Cator MM, VC.

Harry Cator survived the war, became a postman, served with the Home Guard in the Second World War and was active in the VC/GC

Over TheTop! Troops advance on the next objective.

association until his death in 1969.

The next phase in the operations involved the 35th Brigade [10] coming up to the Blue Line, and continuing the advance to the Wancourt-Feuchy line. Brigadier General Vincent, commanding, had his troops sheltering in the deep caves at Arras, and moved them up to the front line area at Zero Hour. He planned not to keep them here beyond 10am, but even by 11am he learned that fighting was still going on ahead of him. Major General Scott told him to go anyway, as he hoped the Brigade's,

> ... appearance on the battlefield would force the Germans, still holding out, to surrender. This Brigade... moving over the top, closed up on the leading troops of the 12th Division. [11]

The 7th Norfolks were on the right, with 5th Royal Berks on the left; behind them came 9th Essex and 7th Suffolks. Lieutenant Colonel Walter's Norfolks wiped out the remaining opposition in Haucourt Trench and the Houlette Work (previously cleared by the Buffs), and 5th Royal Berks outflanked the Holt Work to the north, where the garrison of thirty-five men and a MG08 machine-gun surrendered. Other men from the same Battalion, along with 9th Essex, swept down the slopes of Observation Hill into Battery Valley.

> The whole of Battery Valley was dotted with German artillery: some batteries already abandoned; some, having got their teams up, making off as fast as they could; but several others firing point-blank at the British infantry at ranges of only a few hundred yards. Their blood up, the two battalions advanced by short rushes, covered by bursts of Lewis-gun fire. Two batteries were put out of action by two Vickers machine-guns of the 35th Machine Gun Company. Pushing on resolutely, the Essex took nine guns and the R. Berkshire no less than 22, as well as a number of prisoners. [12]

In addition, some enterprising men of the Royal Berks, along with an attached RFA liaison officer, were able to salvage two guns, change their breech blocks for ones that had not been spiked and get the weapons back in action again. They used them to good effect, dropping shells on retreating groups of Germans disappearing in the direction of the Brown Line.

Thus elements of 35th Brigade had finished the task of clearing the Blue Line by 1.15pm, in some cases were well beyond it, and could now attempt the next move. The ground ahead was open and bare of cover. Aside from a few wired gun pits and one communication trench, Tilloy Lane, which went north east from the Cambrai road right into the Wancourt-Feuchy line, there was nothing but open ground dropping at first and then rising towards Chapel Hill. The Wancourt-Feuchy defences were part of the main Hindenburg Line, and there was a redoubt at Feuchy Chapel. The Germans had been seen to flee, but now were obviously returning. As Lieutenant Colonel Cooper's Suffolks moved up from Maison Rouge on the Cambrai road and 9th Essex came down from Battery Valley, Feuchy Chapel was reached and cleared. However, beyond it was the Church Work, a promontory in the Brown Line. This was well protected by uncut wire, and heavily defended. The advance could creep forward no more, despite vain efforts to get through the wire. Of four tanks allocated to this phase, two had been hit by shell-fire and the others stuck in the mud. Here 12th (Eastern) Division's part in the initial attack came to a conclusion. Its forward elements were installed in Feuchy Chapel on the night of 9th/10th April, while troops from the 37th Division were coming up to launch fresh attacks on Orange Hill and, beyond it, Monchy le Preux. This part of the Arras battle will be dealt with in another chapter.

Major General McCracken's 15th (Scottish) Division operated in the northern area of VI Corps on 9th April 1917. Its plan of attack was similar to the 12th Division, in that it had two Brigades in the front line to spearhead the advance, and the third in reserve to pass through and continue on to the Brown Line; which was likewise the Wancourt-Feuchy line. All the men were well protected in the caves and subways between Arras and towards Blangy, the village situated just ahead of

Soldiers of the 15th (Scottish) Division at Arras 1917.

Returning from the action; troops of VI Corps near Blangy.

the Division's front line. Ahead of them the first line of German trenches dated back to the stabilising of the sector in 1914, and beyond that, en-route to the village of Feuchy, was a triangular railway junction;

> ... this triangle, at the junction of the Arras-Lille and Arras-Valenciennes railways, constituted the most striking feature of this part of the front, and was a serious obstacle. On its southern side the line ran in a cutting, but the lines forming the other two sides were on high embankments which completely dominated the ground between the triangle and the Scarpe.[13]

This strongpoint was detailed to be cleared by the only tanks allocated to McCracken's men, two Mk IIs.

At Zero Hour 44th and 45th Brigades advanced under cover of a twenty-two machine-gun barrage, and advance elements soon took the Black Line, just before Railway Triangle. On the left flank, 13th Royal Scots ran into problems from the start. Two mines were blown under German machine-gun posts on the outskirts of Blangy, and the explosion stunned some of the Royal Scots as they began to attack. Furthermore,

> ... one of the mines did not achieve its object and the hostile machine-guns threatened to hold up our attack even before No Man's Land was bridged. At this criticial point Sergeant

> *McMillan of C Company dashed gallantly forward, and, discharging his bombs with wonderful accuracy, dislodged the Germans from their emplacement.*[14]

With this initial problem dealt with, another company swept through the remains of the village of Blangy, where the attack broke down into house-to-house fighting. Stokes mortars from the Brigade Trench Mortar Battery had to be brought up, and the Germans were seen to wave the white flag. However, when the Royal Scots went forward to take the surrender, the defenders opened up again, and so the Stokes guns rained down bombs until what was left of the garrison finally gave up.

The Railway Triangle was the next obstacle and despite a heavy bombardment, defenders from Grenadier Regiment No 10 of 11th Infantry Division still held out. Their headquarters' dugout was placed here and they had machine-guns and trench mortars to back them up. Positions in the embankment were re-enforced with concrete and timbers and rails from the old track were used as supports in the trench system. McCracken had been concerned about this feature and his worry was proving founded. In the early stages of the Somme battle, artillery plans had been too rigid and inflexible. Lessons had been learnt, so that it was now possible for McCracken to telephone his Commander Royal Artillery (CRA), Brigadier General E.B. Macnaghten, and call the barrage back to the Railway Triangle.

This was underway at 11.30am, just as the only tank to make it up arrived on the scene. The vehicle was a Mk II 'male', armed with two six-pounders, and commanded by Second Lieutenant C. Weber. Weber's tank climbed the railway bank west of the triangle and

Ditched tank on the VI Corps front.

Feuchy church 1917.

proceeded along the track to rake fire into the centre of the position and a narrow strip of trees known as Fred's Wood. The Stokes guns which had bombarded Blangy came up and dropped rounds into the triangle and the position was finally taken at the point of the bayonet by 6/7th Royal Scots Fusiliers about an hour after the first bombardment had started.

Before the village of Feuchy could be reached there was the Feuchy Work at a position called Spider Corner to deal with first. Units from 46th Brigade had come up and passed through the Black Line and over Observation Hill to the Blue Line. As they continued into the northern end of Battery Valley, in an attempt to outflank the Feuchy Work, they had a similar experience to troops of the 12th Division further south. The valley was crammed with 77mm field guns and these fired at virtually point-blank range as 7th KOSB and 10th Scottish Rifles entered the position. There were heavy losses, but the crews were silenced and some thirty-six guns were captured. This opened the way to Feuchy itself and, following a heavy bombardment from 6-inch howitzers, these two battalions cleared the village. They then continued with the momentum and took the northern end of the Wancourt-Feuchy Line (the final objective) with the assistance of the other Mk II tank. A little to the south 12th Highland Light Infantry took their section of the trench system and by 5.30pm McCracken's men had achieved all that was asked of them.

Success on the front of VI Corps had been mixed. Both 3rd and 12th (Eastern) Divisions had failed to secure the Wancourt-Feuchy Line, the only section of it held in any strength by the British being east of Feuchy on the 15th Division front. However, the average advance had been around two miles, which was in stark contrast to the experience of these divisions the year before on the Somme. McCracken, as 9th April closed, felt that his 46th Brigade could have pushed on to Monchy, but he was waiting for the 37th Division, and there was still fighting in the final objective to the south, so a chance was missed. The official historian concluded:

> ... the opposition was not strong in numbers or, apparently, in resolution, but after the first attack of the right and centre divisions had broken down, and the chance had been missed of putting the nearest available troops into the gap made by the left, the April day was not long enough to permit adequate preparation for a fresh operation. During the night only the bomb could be used, and it was not a weapon which could produce quick results.[15]

A Walk in the 3rd and 12th(Eastern) Divisional Sectors

This walk takes around four hours, and covers the area advanced over by VI Corps in the opening phase of the battle. It is a circular walk, starting and ending in Tilloy. Cemeteries referred to in **bold** are described below.

Park your car at **Tilloy British Cemetery** on the D37E. There is an off-road parking bay for your vehicle alongside the cemetery. Take time to visit the graves from the actions of the 3rd Division, then leave the cemetery and turn right in the direction of the village. You pass the chateau grounds on your right and, at the cross-roads, turn right along Avenue Charles de Gaulle. Continue to the main road, D939, and cross it using the marked crossing areas. This road is fast and dangerous, so take care. On the north side of the road follow a minor road and CWGC signs for Bunyan's Cemetery. The buildings you pass are on the site of Estaminet Corner, captured by 6th Buffs on 9th April.

This track takes you due north onto Observation Ridge. Once you have walked a little way, stop. Looking west you have superb views down the slopes towards Arras and the site of the front lines on 9th April 1917. The area beyond the modern factory units is where 37th Brigade made the initial advance. Looking north there are good views to the 36th Brigade area and beyond towards Blangy in 15th (Scottish)

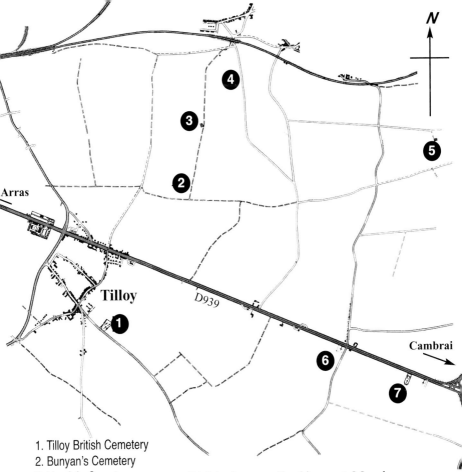

1. Tilloy British Cemetery
2. Bunyan's Cemetery
3. Houdain Cemetery
4. Battery Valley
5. Orange Hill Cemetery
6. Isaacs Memorial
7. Feuchy Cemetery
   + 12th Division Memorial

Division's sector. Looking east, Monchy le Preux and Orange Hill are visible, and using the trench maps in this book is it is possible to work out the site of Sergeant Harry Cator's VC action (see above).

Continue on the track until you meet the next junction. Here turn right and follow this track to the cemetery. This is **Bunyan's Cemetery** and is located just beyond the Blue Line objectives of 12th Division. Trench maps show numerous German gun sites in the area and dugouts in the banks of the escarpment you pass on the way to the cemetery.

Return to the track and turn left. At the electrical sub-station go left on the track, and follow it north to the next cemetery. This is **Houdain Lane Cemetery**. From here there are good views into Battery Valley, which is where the gun sites were taken at the point of the bayonet by units from the 12th Division. The Wancourt-Feuchy Line was located on the lower slopes of Orange Hill – roughly where the factory units are to the east.

Leaving the cemetery, rejoin the track and turn left. Follow it downhill into Battery Valley. You enter it at the northern end where Feuchy Switch trench ran into it. The Railway Triangle is back towards Arras if you follow the railway line with your eye, and Spider Corner is just the other side of the railway bridge. On the banks of the valley here it is possible to see the signs of gun sites, but these are British ones made following the capture of the position. By the close of the battle the heavy guns of the Royal Garrison Artillery Siege Batteries were here firing beyond Fampoux and Monchy.

Follow the metalled road in Battery Valley south to where it joins the Feuchy road. Continue going south, crossing over the area of the final advance on Feuchy Chapel by 5th Royal Berks and 9th Essex. The open nature of the ground is appreciated and, with the Germans in occupation of the Wancourt-Feuchy Line (where the factories are now), it is easy to understand why this attack failed.

Continue to the main road, D939, and cross it at this point to the south-side; again taking care with the traffic. You could extend the walk at this point, if you have the time, by continuing along the D939 to Feuchy Chapel and visiting the **Isaacs Memorial, Feuchy Chapel Cemetery** and **12th Division Memorial** beyond that; you could also see these in a follow up visit by car afterwards. Otherwise, go east for

Battery Valley 2005; signs of the old gun positions and dugouts are still visible.

a couple of hundred yards, and then take the first track on the right. Continue for a little way, then stop and look east.

From this track you have a view across the ground where 1st Royal Scots Fusiliers, 1st Gordons and 7th KSLI advanced towards the Brown Line on 9th April. The attack failed, and they reached as far as a line between Airy Corner and Feuchy Chapel, both of which can be seen from here.

Stay on the track, and follow it right, then left and finally straight on to where it joins the D37E, Tilloy-Wancourt road. Stop. This is the area where 2nd Royal Scots advanced and came under withering machine-gun fire from the Brown Line. Turn right, and continue on the road towards Tilloy, and back to **Tilloy British Cemetery** and your vehicle.

<u>Associated Cemeteries/Memorials</u>

BUNYANS CEMETERY
This isolated cemetery commands spectacular views of the battlefield north of Tilloy. It is located on ground fought over and taken by 12th (Eastern) Division on 9th April 1917. Several units from this Division buried their dead here, and these are found in Row A. Thereafter artillery units, who had their gun positions in the area, used the site to bury their dead, the last burial being made on 4th July 1917. There are fifty-four British graves here, all of them known.

'Funk Hole' near Feuchy, April 1917.

The handful of infantry graves are from the Norfolk Regiment, Royal Fusiliers, Royal West Kents and Essex Regiment from the 12th Division. The thirty-nine artillery burials are largely from 62nd and 63rd Brigades RFA. Among them are Second Lieutenant R.H. De M. Leathes, who was killed on 18th April 1917 and Lieutenant H.F. Hughes-Gibbs, who was killed the next day. They are buried side by side.

Bunyan's Cemetery.

GOUROCK TRENCH CEMETERY
Gourock Trench Cemetery is a mile and a quarter north of the village, some 140 yards from a by-road. It was started by units of the 15th (Scottish) and 37th Divisions in April 1917; one grave was added in March 1918 and four Canadian burials were made in August 1918. Graves total: forty British and four from Canada, four of whom were unidentified.

Most of the 9th April 1917 casualties here are in fact from units in the 12th (Eastern) Division, in particular from the 7th Royal Sussex Regiment.

FEUCHY BRITISH CEMETERY
The cemetery was started by burial parties from 12th (Eastern) Division following the advance on 9th April 1917, and remained in use until the spring of 1918, when the area was fought over again. A few graves were added in August, following the recapture of Feuchy, but there were no post-war concentrations. However, in 1926 a new railway station was built in Feuchy, and the graves in Plot I had to be moved to their current location within the cemetery. Burials total 213 British, with one from Canada. Of these five are unidentified, and there are two Special Memorials.

FEUCHY CHAPEL BRITISH CEMETERY

Feuchy Chapel British Cemetery is on the south side of the Arras-Cambrai road, east of the shrine known as Feuchy Chapel, where a German redoubt stood which was taken by units of the 12th (Eastern) Division on 9th April 1917. The 12th Division Battle Memorial, unveiled in 1921, is close to the cemetery (see below). The cemetery was started by the VI Corps Burial Officer in May 1917, and used at intervals until March 1918, and then again in August and September 1918. It contained, at the end of the war, 249 graves, all in the present Plot I. It was then enlarged by the concentration of 834 graves (mainly of April and May 1917) from the battlefields of Fampoux, Roeux, Monchy and Wancourt, and from a few smaller burial grounds in the area. It now contains the graves of 1,076 British soldiers, twenty six (mainly of the Mounted Rifles) from Canada and one from South Africa. There are 578 unnamed graves, which amounts to more than half the total. Special Memorials are erected to fourteen British soldiers with another six to British soldiers once buried in Feuchy Chapel Quarry Cemetery, whose graves were destroyed by shell fire.

Among the cemeteries concentrated here were:

FEUCHY CHAPEL QUARRY CEMETERY, FEUCHY: about 200 metres North of Feuchy Chapel, it contained the graves of sixteen soldiers from the United Kingdom who fell in April 1917.

GUILDFORD TRENCH CEMETERY, TILLOY-LES-MOFFLAINES: between Blangy and Tilloy, it contained the graves of twenty-four soldiers from the United Kingdom (mainly of the 12th Division) who fell on 9th April 1917.

Among the burials here are a number of pilots from the Royal Flying Corps, who were shot down during 'Bloody April' of 1917. Among them is Second Lieutenant C.J. Pile of 12th Squadron RFC, who died on 29th April 1917, aged nineteen. Pile, flying a BE2c near Monchy le Preux, was killed in an aerial duel with Lothar Von Richtofen, brother of the famous German ace, who himself shot down four aircraft that day.

In Plot I, Row C are eleven graves from 20th King's Royal Rifle Corps, killed on 27th April 1917. They were the pioneers of the 3rd Division, and died in a bombardment while the unit was working on the Cambrai Road close to Estaminet Corner.[16] The inscription on Pte H. Bailey's grave (I-B-8) reads, "Who plucked this flower? I said the master. And the garden was silent". Bailey served with the 21st Royal Welsh Fusiliers and Labour Corps, and died 23rd July 1917, aged twenty-four. Captain R.G.K. Money (III-I-6), 3rd Buffs, who died on 9th April 1917, aged only eighteen, was "one of three brothers, all of whom fell". The family came from Ryde, Isle of Wight.

HOUDAIN LANE CEMETERY, TILLOY LES MOFFLAINES

Houdain Lane was a German communication trench in the Blue Line objectives of 12th (Eastern) Division on 9th April 1917. It connected the Heron Work with Habarcq Trench, and then continued to Battery Valley. It was captured by 8th Royal Fusiliers in the opening phase of the battle, and the cemetery was used at this time by several VI Corps divisions. Two graves, of Canadian gunners, were added in August 1918, and there were no additional burials after the war. It is therefore very much a battlefield cemetery, with seventy-four British graves and two Canadian.

This is a distinct 9th April 1917 cemetery, with all but a few of the casualties being from that date. There is a good cross section of units from 12th (Eastern) and 15th (Scottish) Divisions, and some from the 37th who passed through them. Among them are some of 5th Royal Berks and 9th Essex who cleared Battery Valley, not far from the location of the cemetery, and captured all the field guns there. Royal Fusiliers are also numerous, but from the 10th (Stockbrokers) and 13th Battalions. But there are some of those who fell in the capture of Houdain Lane buried here, including Private W.G. Ball (G-10) and Sergeant A.G. Eldret of 8th Royal Fusiliers. Ball was only nineteen and had just joined; Eldret was a veteran of the Hohenzollern Craters and the Somme.

ISAACS MEMORIAL, FEUCHY CHAPEL

Second Lieutenant Henry Rowland Isaacs was an officer of 7th Suffolks, who fell in the attack between Maison Rouge and Feuchy Chapel on 9th April 1917, aged twenty. The only son of Mr and Mrs Joseph Isaacs of 140 Lower Addiscombe Road, Croydon, Surrey, his body was never found and he is commemorated on the Arras Memorial. However, in the 1920s his parents purchased a plot of land at Feuchy Chapel and erected a large crucifix to their son, set in its own ground. They also bought a house in Arras, and visited regularly until their deaths in the 1950s. Since then it has gradually become overgrown and abandoned.

Houdain Lane Cemetery.

TILLOY BRITISH CEMETERY
See Chapter 5 for a full description of this cemetery.

12th (EASTERN) DIVISION MEMORIAL, FEUCHY CHAPEL
In the initial advance at Arras 12th (Eastern) Division lost 2,144
officers and men. By the close of their involvement in the Arras
fighting, a further 5,000 or more soldiers from this unit had been killed
or wounded. Before the division was disbanded in 1919, it was decided
to erect two divisional memorials on the old battlefields; one at Feuchy,
and the other at Epéhy where it fought in 1918. This one was unveiled
on 24th July 1921, in the presence of Major General Scott, who had
commanded the Division in 1917, and the mayors of all the local
villages. A large crowd of old soldiers from the Division also attended,
and the Last Post was sounded by Sergeant A. Miller, who had fought
with 9th Essex in Battery Valley.

1 Second Lieutenant Robert Mortimer Earl of Shannon. He survived this battle, only to
be killed near Guemappe on 13th April 1917. No known grave; Arras Memorial.
2 O'Neill, H.C. The Royal Fusiliers in the Great War (Heinemann 1922) p.160-161.
3 Ewing, J. The Royal Scots 1914-1919 (Oliver & Boyd 1925) p.402-403.
4 Scott, A.B. & Brumwell, P.M. History of the 12th (Eastern) Division in the Great
War 1914-1918 (Nisbett & Co 1923) p.181.

5 Falls, C. Military Operations France and Belgium 1917 Volume 1 (HMSO 1940) p.217-218.
6 Rutter, O. (Ed) The History of the 7th (Service) Battalion The Royal Sussex Regiment 1914-1919 (Times Publishing 1934) P.119.
7 Moody, R.S.H. Historical Records of The Buffs (East Kent Regiment) 1914-1919 (Medici Society 1922) p.236.
8 O'Neill op cit. p.160.
9 London Gazette 8th June 1917; PRO ZJ1.
10 7th Norfolks, 7th Suffolks, 9th Essex and 5th Royal Berks.
11 Scott & Brumwell op cit. p.101.
12 Falls op cit. p.220.
13 ibid. p.223.
14 Ewing op cit. p.400.
15 Falls op cit. p.225.
16 War Diary 20th KRRC PRO WO95/1405.

Chapter 5

VII CORPS: ADVANCE OF 14TH (LIGHT) & 56TH (LONDON) DIVISIONS
9th /12th APRIL 1917

The Battle

The ground advanced over by the 14th (Light) and 56th (London) Divisions formed part of Lieutenant General Sir T.D.O. Snow's VII Corps left flank on 9th April 1917. Snow's plan allowed for a staged attack, with 14th (Light) going in first, followed by the London battalions, and then 30th and 21st Divisions to the south (see Chapter 6). On this flank the key objectives were the German front lines south of Tilloy-les-Mofflaines, to the redoubt known as The Harp, and

Attack of 14th (Light) and 56th (London) Divisions on 9th April 1917.

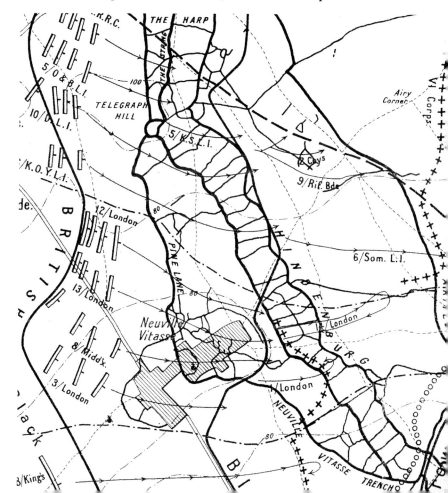

Three signallers of the London Scottish at Arras, 1917.

onwards to Neuville-Vitasse. To the east, the two divisions would advance and take the second line, known to the Germans as *Artillerie Schutzstellung*, and parts of the Wancourt-Feuchy line. The Green Line beyond would involve the capture of Wancourt village, and neighbouring Guémappe.

Major General C.P.A. Hull had commanded 56th (London) Division since its reformation in the spring of 1916. He had seen it through trying times on the Somme, most notably at Gommecourt and Combles, where it had suffered heavy casualties. Hull considered it one of the elite divisions in the BEF, and it certainly had a reputation for getting things done. His objectives for 9th April were 'extremely formidable'.[1] They involved the capture of the forward German positions, followed by an advance to the Brown Line, the Wancourt-Feuchy system. Here they had to capture 350 yards of trench, However, en-route to all this the heavily fortified village of Neuville-Vitasse had to be cleared. Two brigades were selected; the 167th would attack on the right, and 168th on the left. As they approached the Hindenburg Line there would be a halt, and a single battalion from 167th Brigade would push on to the final objective on the Brown Line, meeting up with 14th (Light) Division on the left and 30th Division on the right.

Artillery preparation was aided by the loan of divisional artillery from 50th (Northumbrian) Division, plus elements from a Heavy Artillery Group, including several 9.2-inch howitzer batteries based around Agny. Forward observers on 8th April reported back to Major General Hull that the wire around Neuville was not properly cut, so he ordered further preparation prior to the assault. One of the gunner-officers involved in this bombardment was Major Lushington of the RGA. As zero hour approached he observed:

... April 9th dawned cold and wintry. Heavy black clouds in the eastern sky portended snow and bad weather. They hung like a menace of evil over the promised land, on which the shells were bursting with a slow and languid monotony, as if weary of this endless business of destruction. In the packed trenches, long lines of haggard-faced men, bayonets fixed and gas masks at the alert, waited impatiently for zero hour. In the gun positions, shells were being fused and final preparations made to launch that storm of metal, which like a solid wall of flying death, should move before our infantry, from trench to trench, stronghold to stronghold.[2]

167th Brigade advanced with 1/3rd Londons (Royal Fusiliers) on the right, and 1/8th Middlesex Regiment on the left. Zero Hour was

Light railway system bring troops up to the Arras battlefield.

7.45am and these two battalions were charged with the task of securing the southern portion of Neuville-Vitasse. 1/1st Londons (Royal Fusiliers) would then pass through them in two waves, the first wave heading for the main Hindenburg Line and the second for other trenches and a sunken lane beyond. Finally 1/7th Middlesex would leap-frog them all and move on to the final objective on the Wancourt-Feuchy line.

Lieutenant Colonel F.D. Samuel DSO's 1/3rd Londons did well in their advance, assisted by two tanks. The strong point at Neuville windmill was reached and cleared and by 10am they had reached their first objective just short of the Hindenburg Line. Lieutenant Colonel P.L. Inkpen DSO's 1/8th Middlesex had more problems, first being delayed by uncut wire. In the ruined village of Neuville they encountered a pocket of determined German defenders around the church, armed with several machine-guns. This was cleared with a flank attack, when bombers and riflemen went round them and by 11am sixty-eight survivors surrendered with four machine-guns. These Germans were from the 163rd Infantry Regiment (IR), 17th (Reserve) Division, who were defending Neuville-Vitasse that day.

The original barrage plan had envisaged clearing Neuville in a matter of minutes, so with the fight around the church the Middlesex were now well behind schedule and did not reach the Blue Line until 4pm. However, despite this, 1/1st Londons passed through them without any problems and continued on to Neuville Vitasse Trench, south-east of the village. This was cleared, but at some cost, and when the 1/7th Middlesex arrived to carry on to the Brown Line, they first assisted the 1/1st in the Hindenburg Line.

Meanwhile on 168th Brigade front, the 12th Londons (Rangers) and 13th Londons (Kensingtons) had led the assault at Zero Hour. Smoke had not screened so many of the German observation posts at this point and a barrage caught the leading waves as they crossed No Man's Land. Lieutenant Colonel A.D. Bayliffe's Rangers ran into problems at Pine Lane trench, north of the village, where they encountered uncut wire. A determined German machine-gun team was mowing down the leading companies, and men were forced to throw themselves on the wire entanglements to allow their comrades to pass. These Germans, from the right-flank companies of 163rd IR, held on almost to the last man, and it took a concerted bombing attack led by a young platoon commander to clear the position, just as a tank rolled up and flattened the wire, enabling the advance to continue. The Kensington had better luck, and had swept through to Moss trench, one party of the battalion going to the assistance of the 1/8th Middlesex in the fight for the church ruins.

By midday the Hindenburg Line east of the village was clear, and the next stage of the attack went in. Artillery had come up earlier in the morning to new advanced positions

Observation post near Neuville-Vitasse.

119

The ruins of Neuville-Vitasse.

The scene of bitter fighting on 9th April: the church at Neuville-Vitasse.

south of Beaurains, and the 14th Londons (London Scottish) passed through 168th Brigade and on to the *Artillerie Schutzstellung* where they

> ... *engaged in some lively fighting which lasted about two hours. They killed a number of the enemy, captured 100 of them and one machine-gun, and overran the mass of trenches by 1,000 yards. On their left they were in touch with the 14th Division, but their right was in the air.[3]*

The German defenders from 163rd IR later recalled this position was,

> ... *in short, bloody-taken.[4]*

By the close of the day the Division had advanced some 2,000 yards, taken 612 prisoners and suffered only 881 casualties, despite the stubborn resistance encountered around Neuville.

On their left, Major General V.A. Couper's 14th (Light) Division was facing a similarly formidable task. This formation, largely comprised of light infantry regiments, had been in France since 1915, faced flame-throwers at Hooge and fought through the Somme. Ahead of it at Arras was a maze of German defences centred around the rising ground of Telegraph Hill. Here was The Harp, a large redoubt so-called because of its shape, with a connecting trench known as the String. About a third of these defences were in the operations zone of 14th (Light) Division on 9th April 1917, the rest being the responsibility of the neighbouring 3rd Division.

As part of the barrage plan, the leading waves of infantry would be up to the German wire by Zero Hour, and there follow the barrage up to Telegraph Hill, through the Harp and halt beyond. Here a protective barrage would be placed until the infantry were ready to leap to the Brown Line, or the Wancourt-Feuchy trench. By the time they reached here, the gunners would be firing at the extreme range of more than 6,000 yards, so it was planned to move several RFA units forward after the first advance so that further artillery support could be guaranteed.

Couper's 42nd Brigade would make the attack on the left, with his 43rd Brigade on the right. Each had two spearhead battalions: 9th KRRC and 5th Oxs & Bucks in 42nd Brigade, with 10th DLI and 6th KOYLI in the 43rd. On the left the units would advance on The String, then another battalion would pass through to the eastern edge of The Harp. On the right the initial objective would be the Hindenburg Line itself. Once these were secure, a single battalion would pass through to the Brown Line. 41st Brigade was in reserve, located in tunnels and caves below Arras prepared by the New Zealand Tunnelling Company.

Brigadier General P.R. Wood's 43rd Brigade went forward to the

German communication trench on the Hindenburg Line.

Hindenburg Line assisted by three tanks, which crushed the wire and assisted the infantry. The 6th KOYLI was on his right flank, where it joined 56th (London) Division. This Battalion had been involved in the divisional training scheme before the battle, when units had practised in a system of dummy trenches on the Arras-Doullens road near Berneville. Commanded temporarily by Major W.H. Nicholls, his companies moved forward in platoon formation at Zero Hour and soon reached Pine Trench. From here they attacked Fir Tree Alley redoubt:

> ... *a triangular system of strong deep trenches, very heavily wired. The defences had not been much damaged by the*

bombardment; however, under cover of our barrage, and with the assistance of three tanks, the men were able to penetrate the wire and to capture the redoubt. The enemy put up a moderate resistance only and left about twenty-five prisoners to be taken, a few others being taken out of a dugout afterwards. One heavy trench mortar and two machine-guns were captured; by 8.15 the redoubt was in the hands of the 6/KOYLI.[5]

This redoubt was defended by 76th Reserve Infantry Regiment (RIR), commanded by Major Grüßmacher. His headquarters was in what the Germans called Ochsenwald, or Bois des Boeufs on British maps. His unit reported that the *trommelfeuer*, drum-fire, from the British artillery had reached a crescendo around 5.30am Berlin time, and the British infantry were seen to advance in groups, supported by flame-throwers, something that is not mentioned in British reports.[6]

On the left the two spearhead battalions from Brigadier General F.A. Dudgeon's 42nd Brigade had gone forward, 5th Ox & Bucks having taken the String, following some stiff fighting when the Battalion's Lewis guns and bombers put three German machine-guns from 76th RIR out of action. 9th KRRC, on their left, came under heavy machine-gun fire as it advanced on The Harp, one company losing all its officers. However, the men followed their barrage and the position was carried by 7.50am, the wire here thankfully not proving a problem, being well cut. Three companies from this Battalion then attacked The String, again suffering heavy losses among the officers. One of those wounded was Lieutenant Victor Richardson, attached from the Royal Sussex Regiment. Victor was one of Vera Brittain's friends, and one of the 'three musketeers' from Upingham School, the others being her brother and her fiancée, Roland Leighton. Roland had died on the Somme in 1915; Victor would perish from his wounds received here, and her brother was killed in Italy in 1918. This great tragedy, sadly all too common amongst middle-class English families, has been well described in Brittain's *Testament of Youth*.[7]

At this stage in the advance it was expected that tanks from No 8 Company, C Battalion Heavy Branch Machine Gun Corps, would arrive and assist in the next stage of operations. But 9th KRRC noted,

... by this time the sixteen Tanks told off to attack the 'Harp' should have made their presence felt, and would have been invaluable in dealing with the machine-gun fire from the 'String', but they had all stuck either in or before reaching the front line.[8]

This was slightly unfair, but is typical of the poor attitude infantry had towards tanks at this stage in the war. In fact three vehicles were able to contribute, the others having succumbed to shell-fire or mechanical problems. These were only Mk II tanks, still lightly armoured and with a poor engine compared to later vehicles. The Germans had also learnt to deal with them; one tank from this unit had its tracks shed by the placing of cluster grenades beneath the treads. By the close of the year, at Cambrai in November, the tanks would finally prove their worth.

The final stage of operations began at 11.30am, when 6th Somerset Light Infantry of 43rd Brigade passed through the rest of the Division and made an advance on the Brown Line. No tanks from No 8 company were available to assist, but the guns had moved up and it followed a bombardment towards the Wancourt-Feuchy position;

> ... the barrage lifted and in lines of skirmishers the Somerset men advanced. At this period no troops of either the 56th Division or 42nd Brigade were visible on either flank, which were thus in the air. From high ground on the left of the Somersets rifle and machine-gun fire swept the line of advance and Colonel Bellew found it necessary to detach two platoons to deal with the enemy at this point. These platoons captured one machine-gun and 30 Germans. The two leading companies of the Somersets, however, pushed on towards the Brown Line. About 1.10pm a platoon of the Rifle Brigade appeared on the left of the battalion, relieving the two platoons on the high ground... but on the right the Somerset men were still unsupported and at 1.20pm came under heavy enfilade machine-gun fire from the right flank and rear. This heavy fire was responsible for the serious casualties suffered by the leading company, which was now forced to seek shelter in a newly dug German trench about 600 yards from the objective: here the Somersets set to work to consolidate their position.[9]

This trench was the *Artillerie Schutzstellung*, a formidable looking line on British maps, but which men of the 14th (Light) Division found to be in some places only knee-deep.

Lieutenant Colonel Bellew's men marked the furthest extent of the Division's advance on 9th April. Major General Couper had formulated an attack to take place that evening towards the Brown Line, but battlefield conditions made this impossible. The Corps commander, Snow, intervened and ordered that all available artillery on this part of the front should bombard the Wancourt-Feuchy line next day, followed by a joint 14th and 56th Division attack at 8am, with the 3rd Division going forward on the left. In the event this fresh attack was to start much later, as it proved impossible to co-ordinate all these

Road mending on the Arras battlefield.

formations under the circumstances that prevailed.

On the 56th Division front the London Scottish had captured a section of the Hindenburg Line north of the Neuville-Wancourt road following a bombing attack. The 167th Brigade co-operated with 30th Division on the right, and the 1/9th Londons (Queen Victoria's Rifles) cleared the German positions as far as the Cojeul stream, also taking part of Nepal Trench – part of the Brown Line. 1/8th Middlesex and 1/3rd Londons on the left had been held up by more uncut wire, 200 yards short of the objective, and physical conditions here were now so bad it was affecting movement,

> ... the depth of sticky mud in the trenches was... an obstacle as serious as the hostile resistance. One officer of the 1/7th Middlesex was bogged so deeply that it took two hours to dig him out.[10]

That afternoon 169th Brigade came into the line and began probing out towards Hill 90. It was hoped to advance into Héninel, if the 30th Division came forward on the right.

Units of the 14th (Light) Division had meanwhile finally got a footing in the Brown Line. At 2.15pm on the 10th April, 7th KRRC and 7th Rifle Brigade attacked and, taking advantage of a snow-storm blowing into the faces of the defenders, advanced in artillery formation

A horse drawn Field Ambulance at Arras, April 1917.

and effected an entry into the Wancourt-Feuchy position with two companies. 8th Rifle Brigade came up as well to form a defensive flank, some of its forward posts making contact with 56th Division. The way was now open for a follow up attack the next day.

A combined effort was planned in VII Corps finally to reach Wancourt. Hull's 56th Division was charged with taking out Hill 90 which dominated the battlefield, and threatened the flanks of any advance on the village. 14th (Light) Division would advance from the Brown Line and attack the village. Fighting raged around Hill 90, and Lieutenant Colonel H.C. Bury's 7th KRRC were given the orders to attack, with 8th Rifle Brigade in support. Bury had conferred with his Brigade commander, and both had assessed there was slim chance of success; but the advance was needed. What happened is described in two main sources. The unit's War Diary relates:

… the attack orders arrived and in spite of all protests we were ordered to carry them out. There was no time to copy them and the originals had to be sent up to the forward companies. B and C Companies, supported by 8th Rifle Brigade, were to advance up the valley and try to push on to Wancourt. The 56th Division never left their trenches or made any attempt to take Hill 90. B Company under Whitley made a most gallant attempt to push forward, but from the start it was an impossible task; and the staff who had ordered the attack, if they had ever come near enough to have a look at the ground, would have realised it too, and would never have ordered the attack. Whitley was alas killed, gallant soldier that he was, and his body was found nearest to the German wire which was totally uncut… The whole

affair was a complete failure from want of preparation and organisation on the part of the staff.[11]

The Official History noted,

> *... the attack had no chance of success. Fire from Hill 90 swept it in enfilade; the British barrage was ragged and frequently short, because adequate time had not been allowed for the transmission of orders. The two battalions did no more than reach their previous positions after heavy loss, especially in the 7/KRRC.*[12]

As the fighting raged to the north, from Guémappe to Monchy, it was discovered by 12th April, just as 56th Division at last occupied Hill 90, that Wancourt was now held only by a handful of German snipers. Units from both divisions entered the village, with 169th Brigade passing through and occupying the high ground above the Cojeul stream close to Wancourt Tower. 41st Brigade was now exhausted, and although it was able to establish a position from Héninel cemetery to the Cojeul stream at the south-west corner of Wancourt, relief by 50th (Northumbrian) Division began on the evening of 12th April.

A Walk in the 14th & 56th Divisional Sectors

This walk takes around 3½ hours, and covers most of the area fought over by these divisions in the opening phase of the battle; beyond Wancourt is covered in a separate chapter. Some of the cemeteries are outside the scope of the walk, and should be seen by car in follow up visits. It is a circular walk, starting and finishing at London Cemetery, Neuville-Vitasse. Cemeteries referred to in **bold** are described below.

Start at the **London Cemetery**. Park your car here and visit the cemetery. From the entrance there are good views across the start line areas of the attack made by 56th (London) Division on 9th April 1917. Directly ahead is where the 13th Londons (Kensingtons) attacked, with 12th Londons (Rangers) on the left and 8th Middlesex and 3rd Londons on the right. The dead from all these units are found in the cemetery.

Leaving the cemetery follow the main road (D5) towards Neuville-Vitasse, and then take the first track on the left by a wayside chapel. Stay on this for a short distance and then, at a junction of tracks, turn left, and almost double back on yourself along another track which will take you up to the lower slopes of Telegraph Hill. This track brings you into the attack area of 14th (Light) Division on 9th April and you are roughly walking parallel to both sets of front lines; British to the left,

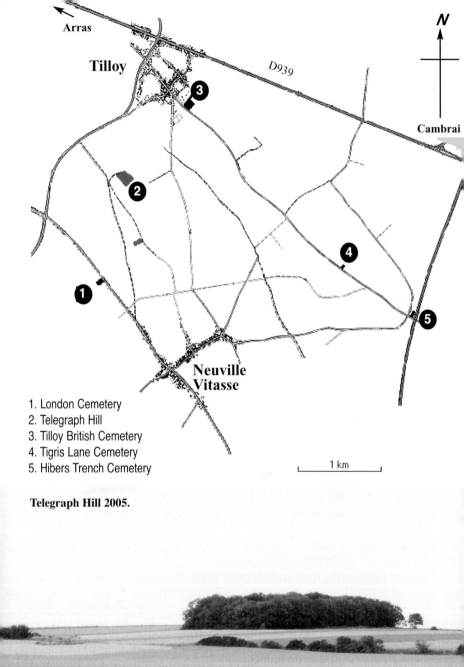

Arras

N

Tilloy

D939

Cambrai

❸

❷

❹

❶

❺

Neuville
Vitasse

1. London Cemetery
2. Telegraph Hill
3. Tilloy British Cemetery
4. Tigris Lane Cemetery
5. Hibers Trench Cemetery

1 km

Telegraph Hill 2005.

and German to the right.

There is a small copse almost on the crest of Telegraph hill. At the end of this track, turn right. There is a track that goes to the copse, which you could follow and return to the main route, to get a view towards Arras from the hill and see the ground beyond where The Harp and The String were located. Otherwise, follow the main track south-east back towards Neuville-Vitasse, which runs between the site of Pine Lane and the main Hindenburg Line trenches. It will take you back into the area fought over by the 56th (London) Division.

The track ends at a T-junction north of the village; here turn left and at the next junction left again and follow past the rear slopes of Telegraph Hill into Tilloy-les-Mofflaines. There are good views to the east, towards Monchy and Wancourt, where the advance of 14th (Light) Division continued. In Tilloy the track becomes a road (rue de Neuville); follow to the next junction and turn right on the D37E. On the outskirts of the village, on the left, is **Tilloy British Cemetery**.

Leaving the cemetery continue along the D37E. This road was roughly the boundary between the advance of 3rd Division on the left and 14th (Light) on the right. There are good views ahead to the distant objective of Wancourt village. Stay on this road until you reach **Tigris Lane Cemetery**. Many of the dead from the 14th (Light) Division advance between The Harp and the *Artillerie Schutzstellung* are buried in this original battlefield cemetery.

Return to the D37E, go under the TGV train bridge and stop at Hibers Trench Cemetery. The ground here is a little obscured by the TGV line and the motorway, but this wartime cemetery contains the dead from 7th KRRC who made a fateful attack towards Wancourt on 10th April 1917. Retrace your steps to the road junction, and take the D34 to Neuville-Vitasse. Walk through the village to the main road (D5) and turn right. Stay on the verge, as this road can be busy. Follow to London Cemetery and your transport.

<u>Associated Cemeteries</u>

HIBERS TRENCH CEMETERY
Hibers Trench Cemetery is half a mile north-west of the village of Wancourt, on the north side of the road from Wancourt to Tilloy. It was started in April 1917, by the 50th Division Burial Officer, and remained in use until the following October; three Canadian graves were added in August and September 1918, and two further burials in the summer of 1919. It contains the graves of 133 British soldiers and

London Cemetery, Neuville-Vitasse.

three from Canada. Six of these graves are unnamed, and there are two Special Memorials.

LONDON CEMETERY, NEUVILLE-VITASSE

The London Cemetery was started by units of the 56th (London) Division in April 1917 and was greatly enlarged after the war by the concentration of graves from other local burial grounds and from the battlefield area between Arras, Vis-en-Artois and Croisilles. Burials now total 575 British, nineteen Canadian, twelve Australian and three Newfoundland. Of these, almost half are unidentified and on a screen wall are panels bearing the names of 138 British soldiers, buried in four cemeteries in the area, whose graves were subsequently destroyed by shell-fire. Those cemeteries concentrated here after 1918 and represented by the names on the panel were:

WANCOURT ROAD CEMETERY No 2: Located just east of Neuville-Vitasse.

NEUVILLE-VITASSE MILL CEMETERY: Close to a German strong point on the road to Mercatel.

BEAURAINS ROAD CEMETERY No 2: North-west of Neuville-Vitasse.

BEAURAINS GERMAN CEMETERY and ERCHIN GERMAN CEMETERY (Nord).

TIGRIS LANE CEMETERY, WANCOURT

Tigris Lane Cemetery (named from a nearby trench) is on the north-east side of the road from Wancourt to Tilloy. It was made by the Burial Officer of the 14th (Light) Division in May 1917 and used again in August-September 1918. The cemetery contains the graves of eighty-six British soldiers and thirty-three Canadian, of whom nine are unidentified.

Tigris Lane Cemetery.

TILLOY BRITISH CEMETERY

The village of Tilloy-les-Mofflaines was captured by British troops of the 3rd Division on 9th April 1917, but it was partly in German hands again from March to August 1918. The British Cemetery was begun in April 1917, by fighting units and Burial Officers, and Rows A to H in Plot I represent for the most part burials from the battlefield. The

Tilloy British Cemetery.

remaining graves in Plot I, and others in the first three rows of Plot II, represent later fighting in 1917 and the first three months of 1918, and the clearing of the village in August, 1918. These 390 original burials were increased after the war by the concentration of 1,228 graves from a wide area east of Arras and from certain smaller burial grounds. The cemetery now contains the graves of 1,445 soldiers and one marine from the United Kingdom; ninety-one soldiers from Australia, fifty-seven from Canada, fifteen from South Africa, four from Newfoundland and three from New Zealand; and two German prisoners. There are 611 unnamed graves, and fourteen Special Memorials to British soldiers. Other Special Memorials record the names of eleven men of the 6th King's Own Scottish Borderers, buried in Tees Trench Cemetery No 2, whose graves were later destroyed by shell fire.

The following were among the burial grounds from which British graves were removed to Tilloy British Cemetery:

ARTILLERY TRACK CEMETERY, ARRAS: in which were buried thirty-nine British soldiers who fell on the 9th and 10th April 1917.

CHAPEL ROAD CEMETERY, WANCOURT: located midway between Feuchy Chapel and Neuville-Vitasse, where thirty-four British soldiers were buried in April 1917.

HARP REDOUBT CEMETERY, TILLOY-LES-MOFFLAINES: located close to a German fort on the south side of the village which was taken by the 14th (Light) Division and tanks on the 9th April 1917. The cemetery contained the graves of thirty-six soldiers of the King's Royal Rifle Corps and fifty-one other British graves.

MAISON-ROUGE BRITISH CEMETERY, TILLOY-LES-MOFFLAINES: located near a house on the main road to Cambrai, which contained the graves of eighty-nine British soldiers, fourteen from South Africa, one from Canada, one from New Zealand, and thirteen German soldiers. This cemetery was used in 1917 and again in March-April and August 1918.

TEES TRENCH CEMETERIES No 1 AND No. 2, ST. LAURENT-BLANGY: located near the Bailleul road, there were thirty-two British soldiers buried here who fell, with two exceptions, on the 9th April 1917.

TELEGRAPH HILL BRITISH CEMETERY, NEUVILLE-VITASSE: on the south-western slopes of the hill between Tilloy and Neuville-Vitasse, this was ground captured by the 14th (Light) Division on 9th April 1917. The cemetery contained the graves of 147 British soldiers, almost all of whom belonged to the 14th (Light) Division and fell near here in April 1917.

TILLOY WOOD CEMETERY: on the western side of the village, containing the graves of eighty British soldiers who fell in April 1917.

WHITE HOUSE CEMETERY, TILLOY-LES-MOFFLAINES: close to a house on the Cambrai road, it contained the graves of twenty-two British soldiers and two Germans who died on the 11th-12th April 1917.

133

1 Falls, C. Military Operations France and Belgium 1917 Volume 1 (HMSO 1940) p.208.

2 'Mark Seven' The Gambardier (Ernest Benn 1930) p.129.

3 Dudley Ward, C.H. The 56th Division (Joseph Murray 1921) p.123.

4 Anon. Osterschlacht bei Arras 1917 – 2.Teil: Zwischen Scarpe und Bullecourt (Berlin 1929) p.41.

5 Bond, R.C. History of the K.O.Y.L.I. in the Great War 1914-1918 Vol III (Percy Lund, Humphries & Co Ltd 1929) p. 865.

6 Osterschlacht bei Arras 1917 op cit. p.36.

7 Lieutenant Victor Richardson died of wounds on 16th June 1917 and is buried in Hove, Sussex.

8 Anon. King's Royal Rifle Corps Chronicle 1917 (John Murray 1920) p.112.

9 Wyrall, E. The History of the Somerset Light Infantry 1914-1919 (Methuen 1927) p.167-68.

10 Falls op cit. p.245.

11 7th KRRC War Diary PRO WO95/1896.

12 Falls op cit. p.261.

Chapter 6

VII CORPS: ADVANCE OF 21ST & 30TH DIVISIONS
9th /10th APRIL 1917

The Battle

This part of Lieutenant General Sir T. D'O. Snow's VII Corps effectively formed the right flank of the British army in the advance at Arras on 9th April 1917. Only a few weeks before, the Germans had retired in this part of the battlefield to the main Hindenburg Line, and

Southern area of VII Corps advance on 9th April 1917.

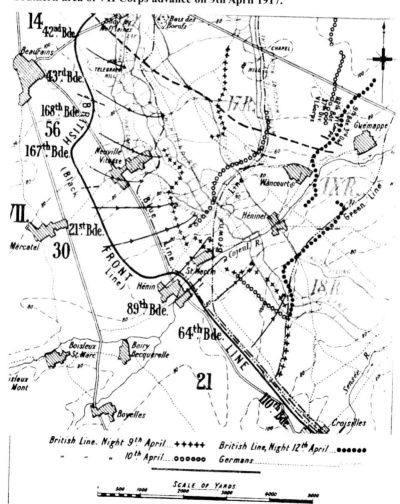

British Line. Night 9th April +++++ British Line, Night 12th April ••••••

"   "   " 10th April ○○○○○○ Germans

SCALE OF YARDS.

Aerial view of a typical Hindenburg Line trench system.

this Corps now occupied parts of the old German front line. Because the new positions in the Hindenburg Line were so strong, Snow developed a scheme where his attacking divisions would advance from right to left, with 14th (Light) Division going first, then 56th (London) Division, the 30th, and finally the 21st. The events along the front of the first two divisions are covered elsewhere in the book, but the plan involved the capture of Telegraph Hill and Neuville Vitasse on this left flank, while the right would advance forward to just short of the Hindenburg Line proper – but not attack it.

The 30th Division, commanded by Major General J.S.M. Shea, was a veteran formation of the Somme, where it had been one of the few to achieve all its objectives on the first day of the Battle. Losses had been heavy in 1916, and few of Shea's originals were left, but most battalions still retained a cadre of experienced officers and NCOs. For the attack on 9th April, 30th Division had two brigades in the line, with 21st Brigade on the left adjoining the 56th (London) Division and 89th on the right alongside the 21st Division. 21st Brigade was detailed to go over at 12.55pm, once the Londoners had advanced, and 89th were to attack at the same time as the formation on their right – at 4.15pm. This was all part of the staged advance planned by Snow. The plan involved an attack on the Blue Line, alongside the Hénin – Neuville road; once reached the next stage was to begin immediately – no pause was to be made. From here they would take the Hindenburg Line at Neuville-Vitasse Trench, and then push on to the Wancourt-Feuchy line beyond. The right brigade was to capture Héninel and, in conjunction with the 21st, to reach Wancourt itself. As a preliminary to the attack, the 2nd Bedfords captured St Martin by 1.30am on the morning of the 9th April. This position afforded greater visibility for the artillery observers, who at daybreak noted that the wire was not cut as required, and called back the fire of their 18-pounder batteries in an attempt to do the job properly.

Brigadier General Hon. F.C. Stanley's 89th Brigade was comprised largely of service battalions of the King's Liverpool Regiment. This was a formation raised by Lord Derby in 1914, and was otherwise known as the Liverpool Pals. It attacked the Hindenburg Line with the 19th King's on the right and 20th King's on the left. The 2nd Bedfords, also part of the Brigade, were in support and two companies from the 17th King's supplied men for the 'mopping up' parties to clear the trenches as the main force went forward. They were all in position around St Martin by 3.30pm and they watched as the 56th (London) Division cleared Neuville-Vitasse to the north. The advance went in alongside 21st Division (see below) at 4.15pm. The official historian later recorded:

> *The men went forward with confidence, but the attack was a failure. It was everywhere held up by terrific machine-gun fire short of the Hindenburg wire, which, into the bargain, was now seen to be virtually untouched. The two battalions, after suffering over two hundred casualties apiece, at first established themselves in shell-holes more or less on the line which marked the limit of their advance.*[1]

Stanley went up to observe the position and realised that any further advance could only be achieved following a fresh bombardment of the Hindenburg positions. As his men were now too close to the objective for this to be possible, he ordered their withdrawal to St Martin.

Henin under German occupation.

Brigadier General G.D. Goodman's 21st Brigade on the left had fared little better. His men had gone forward at 11.38am, with the 2nd Wiltshires and 18th King's Liverpools reaching the Blue Line at the sunken Hénin-Neuville road – here encountering much resistance. Once across it, they advanced on the main Hindenburg Line and came under a terrific bombardment and heavy machine-gun fire. Casualties were heavy, the 2nd Wilts alone losing 342 officers and men in this part of the attack. What men remained were too few in number to effect an entry into the German trenches, and so fell back to the St Martin-Neuville road where they dug in and were later joined by the 19th Manchesters. The bombers from this Battalion were ordered forward when reports, later proved false, arrived at Goodman's headquarters stating that a few men had entered the Hindenburg Line on his front. The Manchesters went in, but were unable to get anywhere near their objective.

The 21st Division was commanded by Major General D.G.M. Campbell; Campbell had been in command since May 1916, and had seen his division through trying times on the First Day of the Somme in 1916. His headquarters for the battle were in Adinfer Wood and his Division held the line from the Sensée river at Croiselles to the Cojeul stream at Hénin – a distance of some 4,500 yards. However, it would

Royal Engineers bridging the Cojeul river near Henin.

only attack along 2,700 yards of this frontage, using the 64th Brigade; the 110th Brigade on the right, composed entirely of service battalions of the Leicestershire Regiment, would hold fast. To assist in the bombardment, artillery from the 58th (London) Division were on loan, and from the Corps assets a Heavy Artillery Group (HAG), comprising three 6-inch howitzer batteries, was also available. A creeping barrage, now commonplace on the battlefield, was organised to be laid in front of the attacking troops and smoke would be laid by the field batteries onto the Hindenburg Line, shielding the infantry from view.

Because of the nature of Snow's plan, waiting for the other Divisions to advance, 64th Brigade did not advance until 4.15pm on the afternoon of 9th April. All through the day the attacking battalions, 9th King's Own Yorkshire Light Infantry (KOYLI), 15th Durham Light Infantry (DLI) and 1st East Yorks sat tight in their forward positions, watching events unfold to the north. Finally their time had come, and,

> ... they moved in section columns, maintaining this formation
> up to the enemy's wire, a thousand yards away, because there
> were known to be but a few gaps in it. The steadiness and
> resolution of their advance across this rising and open ground
> won the hearty admiration of their right-hand neighbours of the
> V Corps.[2]

The reply from the enemy was initially weak; the Germans had called the artillery fire on their positions a "giant steel fist"[3] and the smoke had screened their observation post at Hubertus Farm on the Arras-Cambrai road. As such there was little artillery fire from them in reply and a group from a Machine Gun Company had been sent forward into the sunken St Martin – Fontaine road under cover of the morning darkness. From here it laid down covering fire into the forward positions of the Hindenburg Line. There was a double belt of barbed wire in front of the German trenches; and although some groups passed through, equally as many found the wire still very much an obstacle. Here the Brigade Trench Mortar batteries came up and gave covering fire while the parties of men pushed through the gaps and on to the first trench. Further groups of men then passed through these initial waves and continued on to the second German trench. However, the belts of wire in front of this proved impassable and they were forced back to the first objective.

On the left flank of this advance was 9th KOYLI. The Battalion had all but been wiped out on the Somme, and rebuilt several times. In reserve behind it was its sister battalion, the 10th. Commanded by Lieutenant Colonel Daniell, the 9th reached the German wire and had

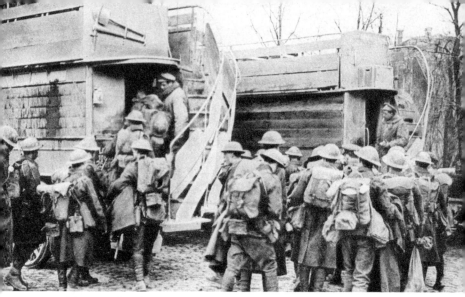

Troops embussing at Arras, April 1917.

likewise found much of it intact. The first trench had been taken, but the second one proved beyond them; the commanders of the two first waves were casualties, and many men had been killed or wounded looking for gaps in the next section of wire, or trying to cut through it. When Daniell himself went forward, he found the survivors of his Battalion dug in around some shell holes opposite the second German trench. He withdrew them back to the first trench and here dug in for the night.

The 10th arrived just after dusk, as reinforcements. Officers and men alike went out searching for and recovering the wounded around the new position, while others from B and D companies organised a new system of trenches along with 126th Field Company RE and some of the divisional pioneers, 14th Northumberland Fusiliers. These new trenches were around the sunken road where Battalion headquarters was located, and a new communication trench was dug from here to the old German front line, now held by the 9th.

During the night the remnants of Daniell's 9th KOYLI withdrew to the sunken lane, with the 10th taking over the line alongside 15th DLI and 1st East Yorks. Part of its front was a trench which led into the next German trench, so a bomb block was established here preventing the enemy from penetrating into the newly won positions. Several counter-attacks were repulsed on the morning of 10th April, the first coming at 8am. They were beaten off with heavy losses to the Germans and much of the fighting revolved around the bomb block. Here Private H. Waller was conspicuous in his gallantry, and was awarded a posthumous

Victoria Cross for his bravery. The citation reads:

For most conspicuous bravery when with a bombing section forming a block in the enemy line. A very violent counter-attack was made by the enemy on this post, and although five of the garrison were killed, Pte. Waller continued for more than an hour to throw bombs, and finally repulsed the attack. In the evening the enemy again counter-attacked the post and all the garrison became casualties, except Pte. Waller, who, although wounded later, continued to throw bombs for another half an hour until he was killed. Throughout these attacks he showed the utmost valour, and it was due to his determination that the attacks on this important post were repulsed.[4]

On the extreme right of the advance was the 1st East Yorks. A regular army battalion, they had been in France since 1914, although few of the 'old sweats' from that period were still with the Battalion at this stage in the war. On the afternoon of 9th April they attacked into a high wind and occasional snow and, although they carried their first objective, they had the same problems as the KOYLIs at the second. During the night they consolidated and the 10th proved,

... a wild day with snowstorms and high winds. Party of 30 untrained men proceeded to transport lines to be equipped and proceeded to front to act as carrying party, leaving at 5.20am.[5]

Having gone into action with nineteen officers and 521 men, when they were relieved on the night of 10th April, casualties in 1st East Yorks had been two officers and forty-four men killed, two officers missing believed killed, one officer wounded and missing, sixty-four other ranks missing, eight officers and 156 other ranks wounded.

On the night of the 10th April part of the line held by 64th Brigade was given up, and when the formation was relieved burial and salvage details went out to recover the wounded, lying out in thick snow and freezing temperatures. It was during this operation that these parties discovered the Germans had withdrawn from the next section of trench and the original first day objectives were now finally taken. Losses, however, had been heavy. In the 9th KOYLI three officers were dead and five wounded; among the men twenty-six killed, ninety-nine wounded and forty-nine missing. Among the wounded was the Battalion's chaplain, Rev. A. Bouchier, who had been with the unit since Loos in 1915. The 10th had lost two officers killed, with three wounded. Other ranks losses amounted to ten killed, fifty-four wounded and thirty-six missing.

The positions gained on the 9th/10th were held until the 12th April when 18th Manchesters crossed the Cojeul stream near Héninel, supported by a rifle-grenade bombardment and support from Lewis gun fire. Here the Germans evacuated about a thousand yards of the Hindenburg Line which formed part of the original Green Line objective allocated to 21st Division on 9th April. In these trenches "magnificent dug-outs" were found[6], which contained a large number of prisoners from 64th Brigade who had been well treated by the Germans – most probably from the 84th Reserve Regiment who defended this ground. These gains were extended by 12th Northumberland Fusiliers, from 21st Division, who captured a further two hundred yards of trench. This was the situation as handed over to 33rd Division, also from Snow's VII Corps, who entered the line at this time and continued the fight further into the Hindenburg Line – but that is the subject of another chapter.

A Walk in the 21st and 30th Divisional sectors

This walk takes around four hours, and covers the area advanced over by 21st and 30th Divisions in the opening phase of the battle. It is a circular walk, starting and ending in Hénin. Cemeteries referred to in **bold** are described below.

Park your car at **Hénin Crucifix Cemetery** on the D5. There is a parking bay outside the cemetery. Take time to visit the graves before rejoining the D5 on foot, and going north in the direction of Neuville-Vitasse. After a couple of hundred yards you will reach a cross-roads, where two tracks meet the main road. Here turn right, and follow this in the direction of St Martin sur Cojeul.

The ground immediately to your right was where the 19th and 20th Battalions, King's Liverpool Regiment advanced on 9th April 1917.

Stay on this track until you meet a cross-roads of tracks at the shrine of Notre Dame de Bon Secours. Turn left, and follow the minor road uphill to the cemetery.

This is **Neuville-Vitasse Road Cemetery**, and from here you have a good view to the west where 2nd Wiltshires and 18th King's Liverpools attacked on 9th April. The Wilts reached the ground where the cemetery is and continued east, but their attack broke against the main Hindenburg Line, which was on the high ground beyond. It was here that they lost more than 300 men, of whom nearly half were killed. Some are buried here, while others were moved to **Beaurains Road Cemetery**, south of Arras, in the 1920s.

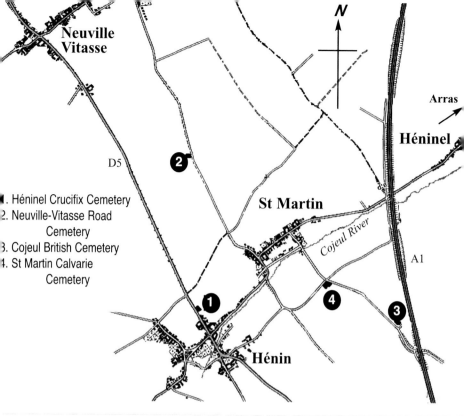

1. Héninel Crucifix Cemetery
2. Neuville-Vitasse Road
   Cemetery
3. Cojeul British Cemetery
4. St Martin Calvarie
   Cemetery

Continue on the minor road in the direction of Neuville-Vitasse, through a sunken section, until you meet a track on the right. You are now in the area where 18th King's were and there is a good view to Neuville-Vitasse village, where elements of 56th (London) Division were fighting around a strongpoint at the church (see Chapter 5).

Turn right onto this track and follow it. It bends right; continue uphill. You are now coming into the area where the main Hindenburg Line was located.

Stay on this track to where it meets another and turn left. At the end of this track stop and look south-east to the other side of the motorway. Here you are looking towards the next section of the Hindenburg Line, the area of operations of the neighbouring 21st Division on the first day of the battle, and the scene of fighting involving 33rd Division in late April 1917 (see Chapter 8).

Follow the track downhill, past the ever busy TGV line and motorway, to where it meets the D33 St Martin-Wancourt road. Go straight across and take the track opposite, following it uphill and right. It reaches a cross-roads near the communal cemetery; turn left and continue uphill to the next cemetery.

Cojeul British Cemetery is just short of the Hindenburg Line, and from here you have a good view of the operations of 64th Brigade, 21st Division, on 9th/10th April 1917. There is a good view back to the start line on the Croiselles road and the open nature of the ground is evident. Many of the casualties suffered here are found in the cemetery, as is the **memorial to 64th Brigade**.

Go back downhill to the crossroads and turn left. Immediately on your left is St Martin Calvaire Cemetery. Having visited the graves, rejoin the minor road and go left, following it into Hénin. It eventually meets the D5, close to the village war memorial. Here turn right, and stay on the D5 until you reach Hénin Crucifix Cemetery and your vehicle.

The memorial to 64th Brigade, which once stood on Wancourt Hill.

Associated Cemeteries

COJEUL BRITISH CEMETERY
This cemetery was started by the 21st Divisional burial officer on a snowy day in April 1917, following the initial advance here on 9th/10th. The bodies of men from the units in 64th Brigade which had captured this position were laid here to rest and Engineers from 126th Field Company erected a wooden cross to the dead. The cemetery remained in use by front line units serving in the Hindenburg Line east of here until October 1917, and it was severely damaged in the fighting of 1918; thirty-one of the original graves were destroyed by shell-fire

Cojeul British Cemetery.

and replaced with Special Memorials. Total burials are 318 British soldiers, of whom thirty-five are unidentified.

On the north-east side of the cemetery is an oak cross erected by the Royal Engineers during the war in memory of the officers and men of the 64th Infantry Brigade who fell on 9th April 1917, capturing part of the Hindenburg Line. The original of this cross was replaced by a permanent memorial in the 1930s, which can still be seen in the cemetery today. The oak cross is now preserved in Beverley Minster, in Yorkshire.

The units of 64th Brigade are well represented in the cemetery. The officers of the 9th KOYLI, among them Captain A.G. Spark MC (D-3), are here, as is Private H. Waller VC of the 10th Battalion (C-55). Spark is one of three officers buried here whose fathers' were parish priests. The grave of Private G.W. Croft MM (C-66) of 15th DLI records he was also awarded the Croix de Guerre with palm.

This relatively small cemetery contains a second VC winner, Captain Arthur Henderson VC (B-61) of 4th Argyll & Sutherland Highlanders, who fell on 24th April 1917, aged 23. His citation reads:

For most conspicuous bravery. During an attack on the enemy trenches this officer, although almost immediately wounded in the left arm, led his Company through the front enemy line until he gained his final objective. He then proceeded to consolidate his position, which, owing to heavy gun and machine gun fire and bombing attacks, was in danger of being isolated. By his cheerful courage and coolness he was enabled to maintain the spirit of his men under most trying conditions. Captain Henderson was killed after he had successfully accomplished his task.[7]

Captain Arthur Henderson VC.

ST MARTIN CALVAIRE BRITISH CEMETERY
Begun by units from the 30th Division in April 1917, it was named after a calvary which stood here and was destroyed during the war. The cemetery remained in use until March 1918, when the ground was taken. Plot II was used when fighting returned here in August-September the same year. There are 228 British burials, of which five are unidentified, and three Germans.

Plot I, Row A has the graves of twenty-five men from 17th and 19th King's Liverpools killed on 9th April 1917, among them Lieutenant

St Martin Calvaire British Cemetery.

G.W. Mason (I-A-1). From the later fighting in 1917 there are several casualties from units in the 18th (Eastern), and 50th (Northumbrian) Divisions. Among these is Captain C. Sproxton MC (I-B-22), the adjutant of 1/4th Yorkshires, who was killed on 19th July 1917, aged 26. A Cambridge graduate, Sproxton was from Hull. Close by is Captain J.E. Brydon RAMC, the unit's medical officer, who died on 27th June, aged 33. A fellow officer of these two, Captain D.P. Hirsch VC (see chapter 8) was once thought to be buried here. A fellow officer wrote home to Hirsch's parents in July 1918 that,

> ... the company paraded and buried him next to the crucifix at Henin. Burton thinks that Captain Sproxton, the adjutant and Captain Dryden [sic], the M.O. were buried on either side of Phil.[8]

However, it seems the fighting a month or so later obliterated any trace of the grave and Hirsh is now commemorated on the Arras Memorial to the missing.

HÉNIN CRUCIFIX CEMETERY

Hénin was captured by units from the 30th Division on 2nd April 1917 and an outpost line was established before the main advance on 9th April. Those who fell in the capture of the village, largely men from the Manchester Pals battalions, were buried in a section of old trench close to a crucifix; thus the name of the cemetery. All sixty-one graves are of soldiers from this Division, the most numerous being Liverpool and Manchester Pals. There are two unknowns, and eight Special Memorials to men whose graves were destroyed when fighting returned to this area in March 1918.

146

HÉNIN COMMUNAL CEMETERY AND EXTENSION

Hénin village was captured on 2nd April 1917 and the cemetery was started by the 21st and 30th Divisions following the advance on the 9th. It remained in use as a battlefield cemetery until November 1917 and a few graves were added in August 1918 when the fighting returned. Sixty-eight graves were concentrated into the cemetery after the war and total burials are now: 190 British (of whom eighteen are unidentified), one Canadian and two Special Memorials. The only cemetery moved in here was Hénin British Cemetery, which was located on the south-west end of the village, on the road running north of the Cojeul stream. It was started in April 1917 and used largely by the 30th Division.

Henin Communal Cemetery Extension.

NEUVILLE-VITASSE ROAD CEMETERY

The location of this cemetery, on a minor road between Neuville-Vitasse and Henin, roughly marks the limit of the advance in this part of the battlefield on 9th April 1917. The 19th King's Liverpools (Liverpool Pals) and 2nd Wiltshires attacked across this ground, and their dead dominate the burials here. The register states the cemetery was started by 33rd Division, but there are few of their number buried at this site. It is possible they did, however, bury those left on the battlefield since the first advance on 9th April. Two burials were made in June 1917 and the cemetery was not used again, falling into German hands in March 1918. There are eighty-six British graves, eleven of

A Great War water tank used by the Royal Engineers still in place near Henin, 2005.

which are unidentified.

Among the 2nd Wiltshires are two decorated soldiers: Corporal S. Merrett DCM and Private R. Skull DCM MM, both veterans of the Somme; Merrett had been in France since October 1914. Their platoon commander, Second Lieutenant S.T. Horton, is buried not far away. All three died on 9th April 1917. The two June 1917 burials are CSM T. Chrisp MM and Sergeant T. Reed, both of 1/8th DLI.

1 Falls, C. Military Operations France and Belgium 1917 Volume 1 (HMSO 1940) p.207.
2 Falls op cit. p.205.
3 Anon. Osterschlacht bei Arras 1917 – 2.Teil: Zwischen Scarpe und Bullecourt (Berlin 1929) p.49.
4 London Gazette 8th June 1917.
5 1st East Yorks War Diary PRO WO95/2161.
6 Falls op cit. p.281.
7 London Gazette 3rd July 1917.
8 From papers in the Liddle Archive, Leeds, and courtesy of Matthew Richardson.

Chapter 7

MONCHY LE PREUX
9th – 14th APRIL 1917

The Battle

Monchy le Preux is a large village situated on high ground east of Arras, overlooking much of the surrounding area and the Scarpe Valley. An action was fought here in October 1914 between the French and Germans, when the 8th Prussian Division engaged General Barbot's 77th Division. Monchy was captured and occupied, and remained in German hands until the Battle of Arras in 1917. The importance of the village was summarised by the official historian,

> ... *the most important of* [the] *hills or ridges is that between the Cojeul and the Scarpe, on which is perched the village of Monchy le Preux. From the eastern outskirts of Arras, from the Bapaume road through Beaurains and Mercatel, and even from the spurs running eastwards from these places, it completely blocks the eastern horizon. When Monchy is reached the view over the Douai plain is endless.*[1]

Monchy's importance, therefore, had not escaped the attention of the British high command and it was realised that in many respects the key to the Battle of Arras was the capture of Monchy le Preux. The village therefore became an objective in the early stage of the advance, being located just short of the Green Line to be taken on day one of the operation.

On 9th April 1917 the 12th (Eastern) Division attacked from the

The battlefield from Arras to Monchy le Preux.

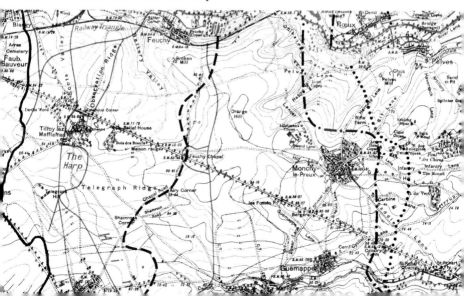

Infantry move up past the gun lines and a ditched tank during the fighting for Monchy.

suburbs of Arras towards the German defences between the villages of Feuchy and Tilloy les Mofflaines. Beyond this area was the main Hindenburg defences of the Wancourt - Feuchy Line, and beyond that the high ground of Orange Hill and Monchy. The Wancourt - Feuchy Line itself was on the Brown Line objective and, despite a terrific bombardment and the sheltering of attacking troops in the tunnel system at Arras, only parts of the Brown Line and some of the lower slopes of Orange Hill were in British hands at the close of the first day.

Major-General H.B. Williams' 37th Division was in reserve at Zero Hour on the 9th April, with his advance headquarters located in the St Sauveur caves. His orders were that once the Brown Line had been reached, his men would pass through the 12th (Eastern) Division and continue on to the Green Line and Monchy itself. By 12 noon on the 9th, his 111th and 112th Brigades had reached the Black Line and, just under two hours later, the 112th continued to Observation Ridge and the 111th went to Battery Valley. By 6pm reports came into this

Brigade that the Wancourt – Feuchy Line was in British hands, but as they came under heavy machine-gun fire it was realised this was not the case. With a flank in the air, unsure of the progress of units around, Williams' rightly decided not to send his troops towards Monchy at that stage.

On 10th April the battle continued, and the units of 37th Division were tasked with exactly the same objectives they had been given the day before; 111th Brigade to take Monchy and 63rd and 112th Brigades to cover the flanks. However, because of the complicated situation on 9th April, the 63rd Brigade actually found itself nearest to Monchy, being located on Orange Hill. It was therefore tasked with clearing the ground between the village and the river Scarpe and the 111th to follow it and attack Monchy directly. Units moved forward, but with some difficulty,

> ... it was found that the only possible method of advance was to dribble small parties forward from one shell-hole to another. This method had to be followed also by companies of the 8/Lincolnshires and 4/Middlesex which moved next.[2]

Brigade observers on Orange Hill reported back to Major General Williams that infantry were approaching the north-east outskirts of Monchy. It seemed the operation was going well and led Williams to report back to VI Corps headquarters that it was a suitable time for

A Regimental Aid Post on the Monchy battlefield under shell fire.

Aid Post established in the ruins of Monchy le Preux, April 1917.

cavalry to come up. A chain of events was started that would lead to disaster, for what Williams and the observers did not know was that the units of 63rd Brigade were indeed moving on Monchy, but coming under heavy fire. Meanwhile, units from 3rd Cavalry Division began to approach the battlefield to be held in readiness for an advance on Monchy-le-Preux.

The 11th April broke cold, but the snow had passed. It was the third day of the battle and a critical one, "… the last day on which exploitation of the victory was attempted on a grand scale"[3]. Allenby, the Army commander, made his intentions clear when he stated,

> … *The A.C.* [Army Commander] *wishes all troops to understand that Third Army is now pursuing a defeated enemy and that risks must be freely taken. Isolated enemy detachments… must not be allowed to delay the general progress.*[4]

Major General Williams had directed 111th Brigade once again to advance on Monchy village, with 112th in support and 63rd Brigade in the valley between Orange Hill and the Monchy spur. Tanks from Heavy Brigade MGC would supply support. The advance began slowly, but 13th KRRC and 13th Rifle Brigade both got a foothold in the village; covering fire from the tanks, although almost all now ditched or disabled, played an important role in suppressing the enemy. The historian of the 13th Rifle Brigade recalled,

> …*The last traces of night were still in the sky when the advance began. With the two leading Companies in two waves, the other Companies behind in similar formation, and four Lewis*

guns to protect the exposed left flank, the Rifle Brigade darted forward through a storm of shells and machine-gun bullets, which soon began to make big gaps in advancing files of men. Wavering, but quickly recovering, the survivors charged over the fore-swept ground, and then up the long slope which led to the village of Monchy-le-Preux, a slope which had defied the heroic endeavours of many other battalions... Now fighting every yard desperately, madly, the men of the Thirteenth gradually drew near their objective until at last that bloody height was theirs.[5]

Meanwhile reports filtered back to 3rd Cavalry Division headquarters that Monchy had fallen. While infantry were there, parts of it were in fact still occupied by the Germans. However, the 3rd Dragoon Guards, Essex Yeomanry and 10th Hussars advanced. The Rifle Brigade could see them.

We saw the cavalry in action – a glorious but futile charge [which] got as far as the village only to be caught, horses and men, in a holocaust of bursting shells. To see those beautiful steeds galloping back riderless, some wounded beyond all hope, was a pitiful sight.[6]

Having reached the village, the units congregating in the main square, the cavalry could not get out because of the heavy fire. Brigadier General Bulkeley-Johnson, commanding 8th Cavalry Brigade, had come up for a personal reconnaissance only to be killed on the Fampoux road. His orderly, Second Lieutenant D.W.J. Cuddeford, recalled,

... The Brigadier thought he would like to see something of the enemy dispositions for himself, and I told him that it could be done, but that to reach the point of vantage on the low ridge in front, the snow having

Brigadier General Bulkeley-Johnson, commanding 8th Cavalry Brigade.

Cavalry move up to Monchy le Preux.

cleared just then, the greatest caution was required, and that if the German snipers spotted us it would be necessary to dodge them by sprinting diagonally from shell hole to shell hole, as we did.

Nevertheless the General insisted on going against my advice, and perhaps being rather old for that sort of active dodging or, as it seemed at the time, too dignified to get well down at the sound of a bullet, he would persist in walking straight on. That of course was deadly, as I well knew.

I led the little procession and sure enough as soon as we reached the ridge a fusillade of bullets hummed around our ears. We had not gone far when one skimmed past me and struck the General full on the cheekbone. I shall never forget his piercing shriek as he tumbled down and rolled over on the ground.[7]

The Brigadier's body was taken off the battlefield, and buried some miles beyond Arras.[8]

63 Brigade was now moving on Monchy in short rushes. Units of it secured the Roeux and Pelves Roads and gradually the 37th Division took control of the village. The cavalry was ordered to go back, being of no further use in a situation that had clearly become static. The Dragoon Guards got away in time, but as other units crossed the open ground from the village back down towards the Arras-Cambrai road, German artillery caught them and,

    ... killed and maimed many, and drove most of the remainder

The cost – results of the failed cavalry charge at Monchy, April 1917.

back out of control in a wild, panic-stricken gallop.[9]

Monchy had been taken, but the cavalry had paid a heavy price. The smell and sight of the dead horses was something that would remain vivid in the memories of veterans who fought there for the rest of their lives. With the village taken, units of the 37th Division were gradually relieved by battalions from the 29th Division over the course of the next few days. One final fierce action would be fought here before the line settled around Monchy; the German counter-attack of 14th April.

The positions east of the village, known as Infantry Hill, were held by 1st Essex and Newfoundland Regiment on 14th April, both of whom were veterans of Gallipoli and the Somme; the Newfoundland Regiment having been virtually wiped out at Beaumont Hamel on 1st July 1916. On this day they were to make an attack into the enemy lines here and, supported by the 2nd Hampshires in the village, and artillery beyond, they were able to achieve seemingly some success – the Germans withdrawing hurriedly. But the whole thing had been a trap; a powerful counter-attack swept into the flanks of the two battalions and while,

... little knots here and there held out for a brief space, [they

German storm troops.

155

were] *surrounded and either killed or forced to surrender, while the survivors, attempting to fall back, were mown down.*[10]

Back in the village, Lieutenant Colonel J. Forbes-Robertson of the Newfoundland Regiment began to realise this was a critical situation, and that Monchy itself might be retaken by the Germans unless a stand was made. Forming up a 'scratch mob' of cooks, officers' servants and anyone else he could lay his hands on, he personally organised the defence of the village until reinforcements from 2nd Hampshires arrived. Forbes-Robertson himself accounted for a number of the enemy and for his bravery he was

Lieutenant Colonel J. Forbes Robertson, commanding the Newfoundland Regiment.

awarded the Distinguished Service Order; later in the war he would awarded the Victoria Cross while commanding a British battalion. All the other members of his party were similarly decorated. These were

The German counter-attack at Monchy, 14th April 1917 (NAC).

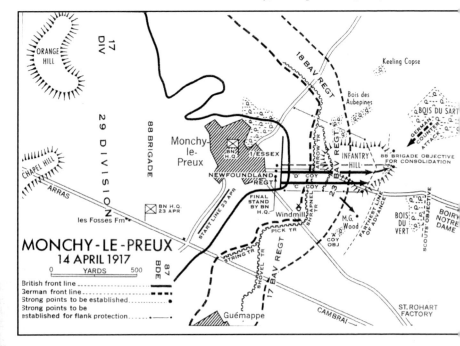

The defenders of Monchy: men from Lieutenant Colonel Forbes-Robertson's party, all decorated for the battle on 14th April; he is in the middle of the back row (NAC).

the men who had saved Monchy; securing the sacrifice of all those who had fallen to take it in the early phase of the battle.

A Walk on the Monchy Battlefield

This walks takes about four hours and covers most of the Monchy battlefield. It is a circular walk, which begins and ends at Monchy British Cemetery. Cemeteries mentioned in **bold** are described below.

Park your vehicle alongside or opposite **Monchy British Cemetery**; there are several suitable parking areas here, taking care to make sure you do not block access to the fields for tractors. There are

The main square in Monchy under German occupation, 1916.

good views across the ground over which the cavalry advanced from here. Having visited the cemetery, follow the minor road that runs in front of it, in the direction of Monchy village itself. Continue on this road. Turn right where it meets another on rue de Tilleul, and follow into the village. Go past a bus stop and uphill; round a corner there is a memorial on the left. This commemorates the 37th Division, who took the village in April 1917. The monument was unveiled in October 1921, when a large crowd of veterans who fought in the battle attended. Originally flanked by two German 77mm field guns, these disappeared in the Second World War.

Memorial to the 'English Division' – the 37th Division.

Stay on this road and follow it along the chateau walls into the centre of the village. The church is on your left; looking at the war memorial in front you will see the village's connection with the Isle of Wight, which

The Caribou Memorial in the 1920s.

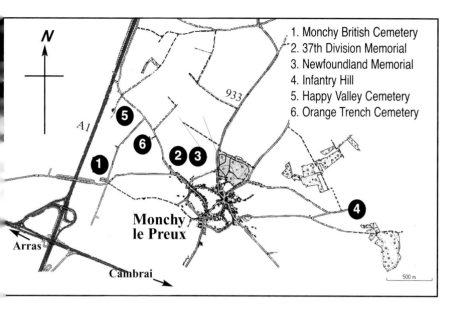

1. Monchy British Cemetery
2. 37th Division Memorial
3. Newfoundland Memorial
4. Infantry Hill
5. Happy Valley Cemetery
6. Orange Trench Cemetery

assisted in the rebuilding of the village in the 1920s. Ahead on the left is the Newfoundland Memorial Caribou. This commemorates the defence of Monchy by the Newfoundland Regiment on 14th April 1917, and is one of five such memorials to the regiment on the Western Front. It is placed on top of an old British bunker, which itself was built into the ruins of a house during the winter of 1917/18. The front cupola of the bunker is still visible, and it was in use by artillery observation officers who had a clear view from here to Infantry Hill, not then obscured by the houses.

From the Caribou go to the cross-roads at the village centre, with a café on your right. Here go straight across past some courtyard gates down rue de Vis. Continue downhill and at the next cross-roads turn left opposite rue Nouvelle, following a minor road out of the village. Stay on this for a few hundred yards, past some old trees and stop where the wire fence ends on the right. From here you have a good viewpoint towards Infantry Hill and can appreciate what an important feature on the battlefield it was to both sides in 1917.

Continue along the track to a fork. Stop. You are now in the area of the fighting on 11th April 1917 when the positions of the 1st Essex and Newfoundland Regiment were overrun (see above). The line defended by Lieutenant Colonel Forbes Robertson and his men was back on the edge of the village; this is the ground caught in the German barrage, and was where most of the Newfoundlanders taken prisoner that day went into captivity.

At the fork take the left-hand track, and after a short while take the turning on your left back in the direction of Monchy. Continue to where the wire fence ends on the right and stop. From here you have a good view, with the village of Pelves to your left, Roeux on the left and the Scarpe valley. In the far distance are the coal heaps towards the Douai plain. Stay on the track until it meets the Monchy-Pelves road (D33E). Turn right and continue. Where the wood ends on the left, take a track following the edge of a brick wall. The track continues, down into a dip. There are signs of trenches and shell holes in the wood, and from here you have a view to the Scarpe river and valley. Coming out of the wooded area, you reach a hardcore track which takes you onto the Monchy-Roeux road (D33). Turn right towards Roeux. After about 1km take a track on the left and follow.

Continue along the track and follow it right in a roughly northern direction. There are again good views from here. As you come over the crest of the high ground the river Scarpe comes into view. Continue, and where it meets another track turn left. Further along another track appears on the left – follow it uphill. This track then goes downhill, and later has tarmac. The cemetery in Happy Valley is visible ahead. The track meets a road where you go straight across and follow the cemetery sign to **Happy Valley Cemetery**.

Leave the cemetery and return to the road. Turn right, and go uphill. At the crest there is a good view of Monchy-le-Preux ahead, a view the men of the 12th (Eastern) Division enjoyed when they reached these

Burying the dead: a provisional cemetery near the main Arras-Cambrai road.

Scattered graves in Happy Valley, 1917. The men these crosses commemorate are now buried in the CWGC cemetery of the same name.

positions on day three of the battle. Continue towards the village until you reach the grass path across the fields to Orange Trench Cemetery.

Leave the cemetery and return to the road. Turn left, then left again at the '10 ton' weight restriction sign down a minor road with Monchy across to your left. This will return you to Monchy British Cemetery and your vehicle.

Associated Cemeteries

HAPPY VALLEY CEMETERY

This isolated cemetery, close to the A1 Paris motorway, is infrequently visited. Happy Valley was the name given by British troops to this position, which runs east from Orange Hill. It was initially behind the German lines at the beginning of the battle, and was reached and fought over by troops from 12th (Eastern) Division on 10th-11th April 1917. The cemetery was started by this Division following the capture of Happy Valley; and was used again by the 4th Division in December of the same year. There are seventy-five British graves here, six of whom are unknown, and one Special Memorial.

12th (Eastern) Division burials are dominated by the Essex Regiment, and the only officer in the cemetery is Second Lieutenant E.W. Rush (A-12) who was killed with 7th Suffolks of that Division on 28th April 1917, aged thirty-two. Machine Gun Corps casualties are particularly noticeable. Five graves from the unique Household Battalion are found here; the unit was formed in 1916 from Household Cavalry Reserve Regiments and was attached to the 4th Division at Arras in 1917. These date from December 1917, when the unit held Infantry Hill only a few months before it was disbanded.

MONCHY BRITISH CEMETERY

Monchy British Cemetery was started following the capture of Monchy village, and remained in use as a front-line cemetery, a comrades' cemetery, until the German offensive of March 1918, when the ground here fell into German hands. Monchy was retaken by the Canadian Corps on the 26th August 1918, and the cemetery was used again for a month. The graves here are very closely identified with the various divisions that fought in this area in 1917/18. Forty out of 552 belong to the 37th Division, there are 327 graves from units of the 12th (Eastern), sixty-three from the 4th, thirty-two from the 15th (Scottish), and sixty-seven to other formations; twenty-three are graves of Canadian soldiers from 1918. There are thirty-three unknowns among them, and two Special Memorials. Twenty-four German prisoners were once buried in the cemetery, but their graves were removed to another location in the 1920s.

Among the most visited graves in this cemetery are the 'Monchy Fusiliers' who are buried in the final two rows. In December 1996, prior to the construction of a new factory, the Arras Archaeological Society were doing some work on the industrial estate, which now sits on the crest of Orange Hill, close to the A1 motorway and TGV railway line. The buildings of it are visible from the cemetery. Here they found the bodies of twenty-seven soldiers, buried in four distinct graves,

> ... It was the burial place of fully clothed men. Soldiers had been stripped of their military paraphernalia, weapons and badges. A few unusable helmets had been left with the deceased. They lay face-up, the upper limbs beside the body or crossed on the abdomen... They were all orientated southwest-northeast, facing the enemy.[11]

However, it was possible to determine that some, if not all, the men were from the 10th and 13th Battalions Royal Fusiliers, both part of the 37th Division who had fought at Monchy in April 1917.

By this stage of the war British soldiers wore two dog-tags; both made of fibre, with one being removed at death, and the other remaining with the body. With the passage of time, all trace of the fibre tags had disappeared, but it was also common during this period of the war for soldiers to have their own, 'home made' dog tags. This usually took the form of an aluminium disc, on a chain. Two of these were found with the bodies, which identified Privates George Anderson and Frank King. They were all buried in April 1998, in the presence of the Duke of Kent, members of the Royal Regiment of Fusiliers and relatives of the two men who were identified.

ORANGE TRENCH CEMETERY

Named after the German trench which defended this position, Orange Trench was taken by the 12th (Eastern) Division on 11th April. It was from here that attacks on the village were made by the 37th Division, and the 29th Division then took over the line in this area once Infantry Hill had been captured. There are 112 British graves, of whom fifty-nine are unknown. Six Special Memorials are close to the entrance.

Burials from the Essex Regiment dominate the cemetery, with four officers from the 1st Battalion commemorated on the Special Memorials. One of them is Captain K.M. Wearne (Sp Mem 3), who was killed on 21st May 1917. His brother was awarded a posthumous Victoria Cross with the 11th Battalion at Lens late the same year. Among the Machine Gun Corps burials are three from the 88th Company in 29th Division. Second Lieutenant W.J. Hutchinson was buried here with Corporal G.H. Hills and Private R.G. Grieve (E-6 to E-8) following their deaths in a curious episode on 25th May 1917. The unit's war diary relates what happened:

> *An enemy aeroplane was brought down very low indeed by the 88th Machine Gun Company... but a shell burst amongst them as they were firing, causing several casualties including four officers, and the plane righted itself and flew away. The officers killed were Lieuts H. Leighton, W.H. Fry and 2/Lt Hutchinson of the 88th MG Coy and 2/Lt N. Grant RFA.*[12]

Curiously Lieutenant H. Leighton was taken back for burial at Faubourg d'Amiens Cemetery in Arras, and Second Lieutenant W.H. Fry died of wounds on 26th May, being buried at Duisans British Cemetery. Second Lieutenant Noel Grant was serving with B/156 Bde RFA and is buried with the others at Orange Trench.

1 Falls, <u>C. Military Operations France and Belgium 1917</u> Volume I: The German Retreat to the <u>Hindenburg Line and The Battles of Arras</u> (HMSO 1940) p.174.
2 ibid. p.249.
3 ibid. p.258.
4 ibid.p.259.
5 Rowlands, D.H. <u>For The Duration: The Story of the Thirteenth Battalion The Rifle Brigade</u> (Simpkin Marshall Ltd 1932) p.91.
6 ibid. p.92.
7 Quoted in 'Senseless Slaughter of Men and Animals' in <u>The Great War I was There!</u> Volume Two (Edited by A.J.Hammerton, c.1930s).
8 Brigadier General C.B.Bulkeley-Johnson, 8th Cavalry Brigade, is buried in Gouy en Artois Communal Cemetery Extension (Row A, Grave 30).
9 Falls op cit. p.266.
10 ibid. p.291.
11 Girardet, J-M, Jacques, A. and Duclos, L-L.L. <u>Somewhere On the Western Front: Arras 1914-1918</u> (Arras 2003) p.103.
12 88th Company MGC <u>War Diary</u> PRO WO95/2309.

Chapter 8

WANCOURT – FONTAINE
33RD AND 50TH (NORTHUMBRIAN) DIVISIONS
APRIL-MAY 1917

The Battle

The 50th (Northumbrian) Division, commanded by Major-General P.S. Wilkinson, was a veteran of Ypres and the Somme. A Territorial division, its battalions had been recruited in the north-east, and it still retained very much a northern identity in the battalions of the Durham Light Infantry and Northumberland Fusiliers. They had been in reserve on the first day of the battle, but on the 11th April began to relieve units of the 14th (Light) Division between Telegraph Hill and Wancourt. The Divisional historian recalled,

> ... *A heavy snowstorm was in progress and the men had been ordered to dump their great coats, taking only their blankets as protection against the weather. All ranks therefore were soon in a wretched condition.*[1]

By 12th April, the new Divisional front was east of Wancourt and Héninel on a ridge close to the Cojeul river. To the left was Guémappe and ahead in the distance Chérisy. The ridge was dominated by the Wancourt Tower, which was still in German hands. As this was an area recently taken, the front lines were a little more vague than usual and it took several days for the Division to establish itself by sending out fighting patrols. One of these was led by Lieutenant Colonel R.B. Bradford VC of the 9th Durham Light Infantry, on 13th April. This

Scene of Attacks on Cherisy. April 1917.

Sketch of the battlefield between Wancourt and Cherisy.

Lieutenant Colonel R.B. Bradford VC, commanding 9th Durham Light Infantry.

much respected and brave officer, who would be killed later in the year as a brigade commander, reported that he

> ... had two companies east of the Cojeul, and two in the river bed (which was dry). Soon after mid-day patrols were reported as having dug-in fifty yards east of the Tower, but heavy machine-gun fire from Guémappe was sweeping the area. Two companies of this Battalion, however, which tried to reach the Tower were held up, and had to dig in fifty yards west of it.[2]

That night, at 10pm, the remains of the Tower fell down, but it still dominated the landscape. Francis Buckley fought at Wancourt with the 1/7th Northumberland Fusiliers in Brigadier General H.C. Rees' 149th Brigade. In his memoirs he recalled that on the 16th April, their sister battalion, 1/6th Northumberland Fusiliers,

> ... discovered the enemy approaching the ruined buildings on the Wancourt Tower Hill, and promptly ordered a platoon to attack them. This plan succeeded admirably and the Tower and house was captured. The place was of vital importance to us as it commanded direct observation on all the roads leading to our part of the front. On April 17 the enemy shelled the Tower with 8-inch howitzers – generally a sign that he meant to attack sooner or later. The Tower contained a formidable concrete machine-gun emplacement, facing of course our way, but by General Rees' orders it was blown up by the Engineers. Sure enough the enemy attacked the Tower that night, and at an unfortunate time for us, for the 7th N.F. were in the process of relieving the 6th N.F. in the front line, and it was a vile night, with a blizzard of snow.[3]

Captain Francis Buckley.

The Tower was lost. Brigadier General Rees at once made plans to retake the position and following, discussion with the divisional artillery commander,

> ... the barrage opened out at the appointed hour, and fairly drove the enemy off the hill top. The 7th N.F. advanced in perfect order and with little opposition recaptured the Tower and the neighbouring trenches. Two or three prisoners were sent down,

who had been unable to get away before the attackers reached them. It was a little attack, but carried out with admirable precision and practically without loss.[4]

With the front a little more stabile and defined, the 50th (Northumbrian) Division began to prepare the area with their Engineers, who made bridges across the Cojeul river to allow access to the front line area. Dugouts were added, and an Advanced Dressing Station made in Wancourt village. All of this was completed in time for the next phase of operations.

On 23rd April 1917 the 50th Division attacked from the ridge east of Wancourt with the objective of reaching ground north of Chérisy and the main Arras-Cambrai road. 150th Brigade was given the task,

Wancourt during the winter of 1916/17.

Wancourt in early 1917.

with 1/4th East Yorkshire Regiment and 1/4th Yorkshire Regiment (Green Howards) making the assault. The War Diary of 1/4th Yorkshires relates what happened as they pushed towards a small copse on the Chérisy road.

> The barrage (a creeping barrage) was very good, heavy and accurate. The German barrage came down very promptly (within 20 seconds)... the battalion suffered few casualties from this barrage... W Company met considerable opposition from rifle and M.G. fire from the enemy first line and had to take up positions in shell holes about 50 yards away from that line. Not until they had established superiority of fire and a tank had come up through them were they enabled to rush the trench which they found strongly held. Many prisoners came out, and the trench was full of dead and wounded Germans. It was a good trench and was not battered out of recognition. Meanwhile X Company reached the enemy front trench earlier and had less opposition... Z Company... reached the first German positions with fewer casualties and less opposition than either of the other companies.[5]

The German support line was then taken by the Battalion, which was found to be full of German dead. But by now casualties had reduced the battalion to a thin line of men and,

> ... enemy rifle and artillery fire had practically ceased, but M.G. fire was increasing in intensity and a particularly deadly stream of bullets was directed on our left flank from the direction of O.19.a [a trench north of the Chérisy road]. Capt HIRSH (now the only officer left) therefore established a defensive flank with half of Y Company. This half company was dug in along a line above and parallel to the river... with the remainder of the battalion (about 150 men) he decided to hold on to this position and send back for reinforcements.[6]

Reinforcements from 1/5th Durham Light Infantry did arrive, along with extra ammunition, but it was at this point Hirsh was killed, and Captain Luckhurst from the Brigade Trench Mortar Battery took over command until he, too, was hit. The survivors of the Battalion held on for some time until around 7.30am, when the Germans were seen to be massing for a counter-attack, and the 1/4th Yorkshires withdrew in good order, commanded by junior NCOs, and fighting rear-guard actions as it went. The battle had cost the Battalion eleven officers and 352 men killed, wounded and missing.

For bravery during the course of this fighting, Captain D.P. Hirsch was awarded a posthumous Victoria Cross. His citation reads:

> *... For most conspicuous bravery and devotion to duty in attack. Having arrived at the first objective, Capt. Hirsch, although already twice wounded, returned over fire-swept slopes to satisfy himself that the defensive flank was being established. Machine gun fire was so intense that it was necessary for him to be continuously up and down the line encouraging his men to dig and hold the position. He continued to encourage his men by standing on the parapet and steadying them in the face of machine gun fire and counter-attack until he was killed. His conduct throughout was a magnificent example of the greatest devotion to duty.*[7]

Hirsch's body could not initially be recovered from the battlefield around the copse on the Chérisy road. It was thought at one time he had been buried by the Regimental Sergeant Major some time later, next to the grave of Captain Sproxton's at St Martin sur Cojeul. However, in August 1923 the Imperial War Graves Commission wrote to the family to inform them that it was believed,

> *... the late Captain D.P. Hirsch VC was buried in a grave about 750 yards south of Héninel, south-east of Arras. As I think you are aware, a cross was erected at this spot on which Captain Hirsch's name appeared, but this cross did not in fact mark the actual grave. As this cross was in an isolated position, it has now been moved and re-erected in the Memorial Plot of Wancourt British Cemetery.*
>
> *A careful and systematic search has*

Captain D.P.Hirsch VC.

The original field grave of Captain D.P.Hirsch VC
(Matthew Richardson)

been made in the area where Captain Hirsch fell, but I am sorry to say that his grave has not been identified. In addition enquiries were addressed to the representatives of this Commission in Berlin with a view to finding out whether Captain Hirsch's named appeared in any of the German Casualty Records or Grave Lists, but these enquiries have also proved unsuccessful. In view of all that has been done, therefore, I fear that there is now little hope of the grave ever being traced.[8]

Captain D.P. Hirsch was later commemorated on the Arras Memorial to the Missing.

Major General R.J. Pinney's 33rd Division had relieved the 21st Division in the right of the line of VII Corps sector around the 14th/15th April 1917. The 33rd were a New Army division which had fought on the Somme in 1916. Graham Hutchison was a Machine Gun Corps officer with the Division, who described them on the eve of the Arras battle;

We were wise men who went to the Battle of Arras. The Somme with its high hopes and disappointments was behind us. Many of the wounded had returned, and those of us who had survived were rich in experience... All things in modern war, its pains and penalties, its ardours and endurances, its few rewards, we had suffered... Renewed confidence inspired us.[9]

The church in Fontaine-les-Croiselles.

For the first few days they slowly edged towards and into the Hindenburg Line, with a number of local attacks in the direction of the Sensée river at Fontaine les Croiselles; but this village remained firmly in German hands. One attack on the 16th April saw 1st Scottish Rifles and 20th Royal Fusiliers (Public Schools Battalion) of 19th Brigade advance on the positions around what the British called Tunnel Trench. The 2nd Royal Welsh Fusiliers were in support; and serving with them at that time was war poet Siegfried Sassoon. The 20th Royal Fusiliers reported,

> ...*Attacked enemy's positions... A, D and B companies formed up and proceeded about 100 yards when heavy machine-gun fire was opened from front and flanks. Progress then was slight and the attack was inching too much to the right. The advance was stopped, and C Company entered the trenches. The attack would have been successful but MG fire was too severe and the attack failed.*[10]

The commanding officer, Lieutenant Colonel L.E. Leader, had been wounded in the fighting, along with his Adjutant. Four officers had been killed, along with seventy of the men.

Meanwhile, Sassoon's battalion had been assisting the Scottish Rifles who had also run into similar problems. Sassoon recalled in his diary,

> *At 3am the attack began on Fontaine les Croiselles. I sat in the First Cameronians HQ down in the tunnel until nearly 6, when I was told to despatch twenty-five bombers to help their B Company in the Hindenburg front line. I took them up myself and got there just as they had been badly driven back after taking several hundred yards of trench. They seemed to have run out of bombs... and were in a state of wind-up. However, the sun was shining, and the trench was not so difficult to deal with as I expected.*

> *My party... were in a very jaded condition owing to the perfectly bloody time they've been having lately, but they pulled themselves together fine and we soon had the Bosches checked and pushed them back nearly four hundred yards. When we'd been there about twenty-five minutes I got a sniper's bullet through the shoulder and was no good for about a quarter of an hour. Luckily it didn't bleed much... I was just preparing to start bombing up the trench again when a message came from Colonel Chaplain (of the Cameronians) saying we must not advance any more owing to the people on each side having failed to advance, and ordering me to come away, as he was sending someone up to take over.*[11]

Sassoon reported to Captain J.C. Dunn DCM, the charismatic medical officer of 2nd Royal Welsh, who would survive and write their history, at the Regimental Aid Post and then walked several miles through the mud to the Advanced Dressing Station at Boyelles. Here he was finally picked up by a motor ambulance and was taken to 20th

Troops of the 33rd Division during the Battle of Arras, April 1917.

Casualty Clearing Station at Warlincourt. This was the end of Sassoon's second period of front line service, and while he was recovering from this wound he wrote his famous protest letter against the war which was published in *The Times*. Sassoon returned to the Western Front in 1918 and was wounded for a second time on the Arras front.

However, the High Command now planned a major continuation of the Arras Offensive, to begin on 23rd April 1917, known as the Second Battle of the Scarpe. The role of the 33rd Division in this operation was for 100th Brigade (Brigadier General A.W.F. Baird) to secure a position east of the Sensée river, and 98th Brigade (Brigadier General D. Heriot Maitland) was to fight to a position near a stream that bordered the Hindenburg Line. Being part of a larger operation, the success of the party which would cross the Sensée depended on the result of fighting on either flank of the Division, but,

> ... the advance down the Hindenburg Line had hitherto been painfully slow and costly, so that it appeared necessary to give it some aid by means of a subsidiary operation of this sort.[12]

The 1st Queens would make this advance on the Sensée, supported by two companies from 16th King's Royal Rifle Corps (Church Lads Brigade), and supported by tanks. However, both tanks broke down and took no part in the battle and much of the wire was found to be uncut by the barrage. The front line positions on the main Hindenburg Line were breached by 1st Queen's but, because of the uncut state of the wire on the support line, no entry could be made there and the fighting got bogged down in bombing and bayonet attacks by both sides. The remaining parties of the Queens and KRRC held on until 1.55pm and were then forced back following a determined German counter-attack protected by trench mortar fire and led by storm-troops. A large number of British prisoners were taken by the Germans in this battle, which costs 1st Queens 118 dead alone and 16th KRRC ten officers and 260 men killed, wounded and missing.[13]

Graham Hutchison had been taking part in these operations with his Machine Gun Company. He had gone forward with 1st Queens and 16th KRRC and was in a post before Fontaine les Croiselles.

> *A chalk quarry lay under the Hindenburg Line, and here I had my command post, within thirty yards of the machine-gun battery, hailing lead at the two-storied concrete machine-gun nests and sweeping the German supports. In this quarry, too, had been herded some two hundred prisoners, taken during the first success of the assault. At this hour of desperation I sent my*

groom, tucked on the saddle of my charger, through the tempest of the Sensée Valley, with a message reporting the position to the Brigade. At the same time I called for a volunteer to drive a limber loaded with bombs up the valley and into the Hindenburg Line. That story is one of the most heroic in all the history of mules and drivers. The body of the driver was riddled with shot. The mule itself, with its load, toppled into the besieged trench. But in that instant the Germans made a determined counter-attack, driving the remaining elements of the Queens and Rifles from the Hindenburg Line. As the men came back the well-posted enemy machine-guns picked them off like rabbits in a battue, and scarcely a man returned unwounded. After this first assault, the 1st Queens... numbered less than one hundred men.[14]

Meanwhile 98th Brigade were fighting in the next section of the Hindenburg Line with three battalions in the line; 1/4th Suffolks, 2nd Argyll and Sutherland Highlanders, and 1st Middlesex. What happened to the 2nd Argylls is explained in their War Diary:

The 2nd A & S H advanced [at 4.45am] in two waves of 2 platoons each at 50 yards interval, and the support moved up into our original front line. At 4.49am, A Company and 1 platoon of B Company had reached their first objective. The other 3 platoons of B Company were checked by machine-gun fire from the Copse at N.36.c.73. A Company and 1 platoon of B Company continued their advance under our barrage to their final objective... which was well over the crest of the ridge looking down on Fontaine les Croiselles. Two platoons of D Company were sent forward to reinforce the platoon of B Company which was held up, but were unable to make further progress.

A message timed 6.20am was received... saying that the final objective had been captured and was being consolidated and that touch had been established with Middlesex on the left and Suffolks on our right.

About 10am the Germans heavily counter-attacked the Suffolks, and drove back the companies in the Hindenburg Support Line to their original positions. This left the right flank of A Company unprotected. The 30th Division had failed to reach the final objective on our left at an early stage in the operations so that the elements of 2nd A & S H and Middlesex Regiment in the final objective had both flanks exposed and had Germans in the Copse to the rear of them,

About 11am the Germans bombed the trench leading from the

Hindenburg Support Line to the sunken road east of the Copse, thus completely cutting all communication with the Companies in the final objective. The situation remained in this critical state till about 6pm. At 6pm a renewed artillery bombardment was opened on the original objective and at 6.24 a fresh attack was launched by two companies Royal Welsh Fusiliers supported by the details of Middlesex and A & S H who had been in reserve to the first attack. This attack was a failure and the trench in which the reserve details were was organised for defence.[15]

Reinforcements from the Scottish Rifles arrived in the early evening, and next morning orders were given for a total withdrawal back to Brigade Support positions beyond Héninel. However, some patrols from 2nd Royal Welsh Fusiliers reported back that some survivors from 2nd Argylls and 1st Middlesex were still in the original objective in front of Fontaine. Given that it was now daylight it was impossible to withdraw them back over the skyline, which was in full view of the enemy. They therefore stayed in these exposed positions until dusk, and finally rejoined the rest of the Battalion at 11.30pm. Losses amounted to 14 officers (including the commanding officer, Lieutenant Colonel C.B.J. Riccard, wounded) and more than 250 men killed, wounded and missing. In the 1st Middlesex it was a similar story. Out of just over 400 officers and men who had gone into battle, thirteen officers and 169 men had become casualties.[16]

For the continuation of the Arras offensive on 3rd May 1917, the 33rd Division were still in the line opposite Fontaine. However, they played no major part in these operations, but witnessed the unsuccessful attempt to take Fontaine by the 21st Division on their left, which resulted in heavy casualties. While Fontaine remained firmly in German hands for the rest of the battle, the last action fought here by the 33rd Division was when 19 and 100 Brigades assaulted the German lines on 20th May. The *War Diary* of 4th King's Liverpool Regiment explains what happened.

33rd Division attack along the Hindenburg Line, the battalion was engaged on bombing down the Hindenburg Line in conjunction with an attack made by the 19th and 100th Brigades. The attack was successful.[17]

Successful, but with the loss to this Battalion of five officers killed, three wounded, and sixteen men killed and seventy-nine wounded. The Official History noted of this operation,

… The Hindenburg Line… was by now battered almost out of recognition… The outcome of the series of operations was the

The ruins of Wancourt Tower, 2005

capture of the front Hindenburg Line on a frontage of a mile and a quarter and of the support trench for over half that distance, with about 220 prisoners, but at a cost of upwards of 2,000 casualties. The attacks had been conducted with skill... but too much was asked of the troops.[18]

A Walk on the Wancourt Battlefield

This walk takes around 3½ hours, and covers most of the area fought over by the 33rd and 50th Divisions in the fighting for Wancourt and Fontaine. It is a circular walk, beginning and ending at Wancourt. Cemeteries referred to in **bold** are described below.

Park your vehicle near to **Wancourt British Cemetery**. There is good parking alongside a small football field close by. After visiting the cemetery retrace your steps and take the minor road uphill. As you reach the summit

1. Wancourt British Cemetery
2. Wancourt Tower
3. Bootham Cemetery
4. Chérisy Road East Cemetery
5. Rookery British Cemetery
6. Cojeul Passage Cemetery
7. Héninel-Croissles Communal Cemetery

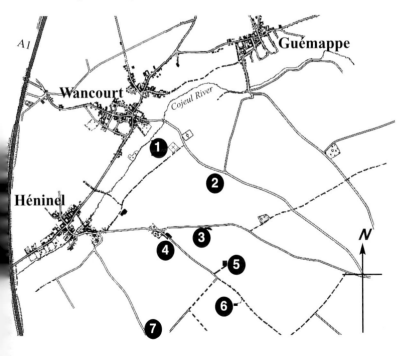

177

you will see on the right the remains of Wancourt Tower. The views from here are very good indeed, and it is easy to appreciate the importance of this location in 1917; Wancourt, Guémappe, Chérisy and Monchy are all visible. Past the remains of the Tower, take the minor road/track on the left and follow towards Guémappe. As it drops downhill, the track joins the Guémappe-Chérisy road. Turn right and follow this to the small copse, to the left of the road.

This is the ground fought over by 150 Brigade on 23rd April 1917, and was where Captain D.P. Hirsch of 1/4th Yorkshire Regiment carried out the series of deeds that won him a Victoria Cross and cost him his life that day. Continue past the copse and take the next track on the right. Follow this across the minor Wancourt-Chérisy road and past another small copse on your right until you meet the Héninel Chérisy road. Turn right and continue to **Bootham Cemetery**.

The view towards the wood where Captain D. P. Hirsch won his VC, 2005.

Leaving the cemetery, continue along the road to the outskirts of Héninel. Take the road to the left in an area of scattered trees and follow to **Chérisy Road East Cemetery**. From here continue along the road and then follow the path to **Rookery British Cemetery**. Returning along the path, go left and follow the track to **Cuckoo Passage Cemetery**. Return along the track towards Rookery Cemetery and take the first track on the left. This will take you straight to **Héninel-Croiselles Road Cemetery**. Approaching the cemetery you will see signs of concrete bunkers in the fields, part of the Hindenburg Line defences.

From the cemetery take the minor road towards Héninel. This will take you through the area where 33rd Division was fighting in April 1917; about half way along you will be close to where Siegfried Sassoon was wounded on 16th April with 2nd Royal Welsh Fusiliers. Stay on the road into the outskirts of Héninel, following it round a bend. Here turn right, going back uphill for a very short way until you see a track on the left; follow this to **Héninel Communal Cemetery Extension**.

From here stay on this track, which will lead you back to Wancourt British Cemetery and your vehicle.

Héninel Communal Cemetery Extension.

Associated Cemeteries

BOOTHAM CEMETERY

Bootham Cemetery was named from a nearby trench, which itself was named after Bootham School in Yorkshire. Burials were first made here in April 1917, largely by the 56th (London) Division Burial Officer. It contains the graves of 186 soldiers from the United Kingdom, of whom seventy-one served with 2nd Royal Scots Fusiliers and forty-four with the 16th Londons (Queen's Westminster Rifles); the remaining seventy-one were not identified. One German grave has been removed to another cemetery.

2nd Royal Scots Fusiliers from 33rd Division had taken part in an attack on the Hindenburg Line on 23rd April 1917, when it lost more than 150 officers and men killed. The burials here account for nearly half that number, including two of their officers and an old soldier, Private C. Fyfe (C-40) who was killed on 23rd April, aged forty-four. The Queen's Westminster Rifles had lost three officers and eighty-six men killed in their action near Héninel on 14th April 1917; again nearly half of their dead from that day are buried here. Rifleman R.H. Batten (A-5) of the Battalion fell that day, aged nineteen. The inscription on his grave reads, "Sudden death, sudden glory".

CHÉRISY ROAD EAST CEMETERY, HÉNINEL

Chérisy Road East Cemetery was started by Burial Officers of the 30th and 33rd Divisions in late April 1917. There are eighty-two British soldiers buried here, nineteen of whom are unknowns. The cemetery is

Cuckoo Passage Cemetery's in one of the quietest and loneliest places on the battlefield; it is also one of the most poignant cemeteries.

largely, if not completely, a 'collective grave' or 'trench grave' with more than one name on most of the headstones. The majority of the burials are from the Liverpool and Manchester Pals battalions of 30th Division, who died near Héninel between 23rd/28th April 1917. Among them is a regular soldier of the Manchesters, Company Sergeant Major P.J. Bailey (Grave 39), who had served before the war, but was with the 16th Manchesters (Pals) when he died on 23rd April 1917, aged twenty-seven.

CUCKOO PASSAGE CEMETERY
The cemetery was named after a trench which ran from north-east to south-west beside the site of the current cemetery. Started by a Divisional Burial Officer (almost certainly from the 30th Division) in late April 1917, it was closed the following month. There are fifty-four British soldiers buried here, of whom forty-one served with the Manchester Regiment; one soldier is unknown.

Sunken road near Héninel – once lined with dugouts and in the thick of the fighting in April 1917.

The Manchester burials at Cuckoo Passage are all from the Manchester Pals battalions of 30th Division, which makes it very much a comrades' cemetery where men who served and fought together, are buried together.

GUÉMAPPE BRITISH CEMETERY

Guémappe was captured by elements of the 15th (Scottish) Division on 23rd/24th April 1917, twelve days after Wancourt. It was lost on 23rd March 1918, and then retaken by the Canadian Corps advance on 26th August. Guémappe British Cemetery is on the road to Wancourt, opposite the junction to Monchy le Preux. It was started by battalions of the 15th (Scottish) Division after the capture of Guémappe, and used by front line units until January 1918 but was badly damaged by shell-fire in March – August 1918. The cemetery contains the graves of 169 British soldiers, of whom 112 served with the 8th Seaforth Highlanders and the 9th Black Watch. There are six unnamed graves.

In Plot I, Rows B, C and D are the majority of the original burials from the fighting for Guémappe in April 1917. Among these is CSM J.C. Campbell (I-D-23), of the 8th Seaforths, who was killed on 23rd

April 1917, aged twenty-five. Plot I, Row E unusually contains a large officers' plot with the majority of officer casualties from the Seaforths and Black Watch who fell on 23rd April.

HÉNINEL COMMUNAL CEMETERY EXTENSION
Héninel was captured on 12th April 1917, in a snowstorm, by elements of both the 56th (London) and 21st Divisions. The 50th (Northumbrian) Division, advancing from Héninel over the next couple of days, captured the nearby Wancourt Tower, which became a pivotal position on the battlefield. Héninel Communal Cemetery Extension is on the south-west side of the civilian communal cemetery, east of the village. It was started by the 50th Division Burial Officer in April 1917, and used by front line units around Héninel and Wancourt until the following November. Burials total: 140 British soldiers, of whom seven are unidentified.

Rows A and B are roughly in date order, and include the majority of burials from the 50th Division operations in April – May 1917. The 18th (Eastern) Division then used the cemetery, and two officers from 7th Queens are among the burials. Captain Valentine Hook (B-18) and Captain H.R. Longbourne DSO (B-17) both died on 3rd May 1917. Hook was only twenty-one, but had been mentioned in despatches, and was educated at Westminster School. Longbourne had been decorated on the Somme, and was thirty-three. The register records that he "… raised A Company in Hunts Cyclist Battalion February 1914, transferred to the Queens 1916". From Rispley in Sussex, the inscription on his grave reads, "Thy noble example liveth".

HÉNINEL – CROISELLES ROAD CEMETERY
The 21st Division captured Héninel on the 12th April 1917, and then

Héninel-Croiselles Road Cemetery, close to where war poet Siegfried Sassoon was wounded in April 1917.

continued their advance eastwards over the next few days. The 33rd Division then took over the line south of the village. Both of these divisions are greatly represented by the burials in this cemetery. In March 1918 Héninel was lost and the eleven German graves in Plot I, Rows D and E, were made when the cemetery was in German hands. After the war, ninety-three graves were brought in from a wide area round Héninel. Burials total: 297 British soldiers, ten Australian, and eleven German. Some 104 of the British graves are unidentified.

The burials here are dominated by the 33rd Division action on 23rd April 1917, in particular by men from 2nd Argyll and Sutherland Highlanders, 5th Scottish Rifles, 1st Middlesex and 20th Royal Fusiliers (Public Schools). Among them are the majority of the officers from these units who fell in this action. Second Lieutenant G.L.J. Baker (I-B-2), 1st Middlesex, died aged twenty, and was a "former medical student... and a former Captain of Sherborne School Rugby XV". Second Lieutenant A.R. Henry (I-B-1) of the same battalion was thirty three and the inscription on his grave reads, "He died a hero, admired by his officers, admired by his men".

ROOKERY BRITISH CEMETERY

The cemetery was named after a group of trenches that were close by and was started by the Burial Officers of the 18th (Eastern) and the 50th (Northumbrian) Divisions between April and June 1917. It was used until November 1917 and the last two burials were made in August 1918. Graves total: fifty-five British, one of whom is unknown. The original register recorded that "it stands over dug-outs and subterranean galleries, and therefore no Cross or wall is erected".

This is very much a comrades' cemetery, like Cuckoo Passage which is close by. Nearly a quarter of the graves are men from 6th Northants who died in the first few days of June 1917, during a tour of the trenches in front of Chérisy. The 1/4th Yorkshire Regiment also have a number of burials in this cemetery, among them one of their Company Sergeant Majors, F.J. Hopper (A-14), who died on 27th June 1917, aged thirty-two.

WANCOURT BRITISH CEMETERY

Wancourt was captured on 12th April 1917 following heavy fighting, and the advance was continued over the course of the following days. The cemetery was opened about ten days later. It was started by units from the 50th (Northumbrian) Division, and by the close of the war, within the cemetery, the following units had all erected wooden crosses

Rookery British Cemetery.

to their dead: 1/4th and 1/5th Yorkshire Regiment, 1/5th and 1/6th
Durham Light Infantry, 1/5th Border Regiment and the 1/6th
Northumberland Fusiliers. It was called at first Cojeul Valley
Cemetery, or River Road Cemetery, and was used until October 1918,
when Row D of Plot III was then the last row. However, it was in
German hands from March 1918 until the 26th August, when the
Canadian Corps recaptured Wancourt. At the close of the war it was a
cemetery of some 410 graves, but post war it was very greatly
increased by the concentration of 1,429 graves from small cemeteries
and isolated positions on the battlefields around Arras. Burials total:
1,026 British graves (of whom 238 are unidentified), 246 Canadian (of
whom 24 are unidentified), one from Bermuda and 566 whose name
and unit unknown. There are Special Memorials to seventy-six British
soldiers and in addition the names of twenty who were buried in Signal

Trench Cemetery and whose graves were destroyed later in the war are commemorated on other Special Memorials.

Among the cemeteries concentrated into Wancourt were the following:

ST. MARTIN-CROISILLES ROAD CEMETERY: located in St Martin sur Cojeul. In this cemetery, about midway on the road, were buried fifteen British officers and men who fell on the 9th April 1917, or on the four following days, and of whom thirteen belonged to the 1st East Yorks.

SHAFT TRENCH CEMETERY: located in Héninel, about a mile from that village on the road to Croiselles. Here, in April, May and June 1917, nineteen British soldiers were buried by units from the 50th (Northumbrian) Division.

SIGNAL TRENCH CEMETERY, HÉNINEL: here, on the further side of the ridge between Wancourt and Chérisy, 'in a rather broken part of the British front line', twenty-two British soldiers were buried in April and May 1917.

FONTAINE ROAD CEMETERY, HÉNINEL: in this cemetery, slightly north of Signal Trench Cemetery, seventeen British officers and men (mainly from 2nd Royal Welch Fusiliers) were buried in April 1917.

HÉNINEL-CHÉRISY ROAD WEST CEMETERY, HÉNINEL: which was about half a mile east of Héninel village, and contained twenty-five British graves from April 1917.

THE LINCOLNS CEMETERY, ST MARTIN-SUR-COJEUL: about a mile south-east of that village, where twenty-two men of the 1st Lincolns, who died on 11th April 1917, were buried.

HÉNIN NORTH CEMETERY, HÉNIN-SUR-COJEUL: about a mile north of the village, containing the graves of twenty-nine British soldiers who fell on 9th April 1917, and almost all of whom belonged to the 2nd Wiltshires or the 18th King's Liverpools of the 30th Division.

Unlike any other cemetery on the Western Front, Wancourt British Cemetery could be called the 'Machine Gun Corps' graveyard. There are a large number of MGC graves here, sadly many of them unknown. They include, however, two members of the Heavy Branch, who were then manning the tanks which operated on the Arras battlefield in 1917. Second Lieutenant F.A. Rankin (I-D-23) and Gunner J. Miller (I-D-23, the same grave), were both in a tank of D Battalion HB MGC when they were killed south of Guémappe on 23rd April 1917. The unit War Diary relates what happened,

'Tanks experienced some difficulty in observation owing to mist and tank No D11 received a direct hit and caught fire at O.19.a.83. Lieutenant Rankin and one O.R. being burnt in tank.'[19]

Rankin had enlisted in the 10th King's Liverpools (Liverpool Scottish) in August 1914 and then was commissioned into the 1/5th Border Regiment before transferring to the MGC.

Cavalry graves from the action around Monchy are also found here, among them Captain M.L. Yeatfield (IV-D-3), 12th Lancers, who was killed on 11th April 1917, aged thirty-three. Yeatfield was a regular who had been commissioned in April 1903 and his father was a Lieutenant Colonel who commanded 2nd King's Own Royal Lancaster Regiment. RSM S.T. Daly (IV-E-11) served with 12th West Yorks, and was killed on 13th April 1917, aged twenty-seven. Sergeant P.J. Farrell (VI-G-3) was one of the Bermuda Rifle Volunteer Corps who served with 1st Lincolns on the Western Front. He was killed on 11th April 1917, aged thirty-nine, and was from Spanish Point, Bermuda. The headstone of Major Henry Archer Johnstone (VIII-A-5), 152nd Royal Field Artillery, records a family tragedy. The inscription records that his brothers Second Lieutenant William McCall Johnstone and Sergeant J.G. Johnstone, both died in the war. Henry was killed with his unit on 21st March 1918. William died with the same unit in February 1916, and the final brother died of war wounds in May 1922.

1 Wyrall, E. The Fiftieth Division 1914-1919 (Naval & Military Press reprint 1999) p.206.
2 ibid. p.208.
3 Buckley, F. Q.6.A. and Other Places: Recollections of 1916, 1917, 1918 (Spottiswoode 1920) p.130.
4 ibid. p.131.
5 War Diary 4th Yorkshire Regiment, supplied by Matthew Richardson.
6 ibid.
7 London Gazette 14th June 1917, PRO ZJ1.
8 From private papers supplied by Matthew Richardson.
9 Hutchison, G.S. Warrior (Hutchinson c.1930) p.178-179.
10 War Diary 20th Royal Fusiliers PRO WO95/2423.
11 Hart-Davies, R.(Ed) Siegfried Sassoon Diaries 1915-1918 (Faber & Faber 1983) p.155.
12 Falls, C. Military Operations France and Belgium 1917 Volume 1 (HMSO 1940) p.384.
13 Anon. The King's Royal Rifle Corps Chronicle 1917 (John Murray 1920) p. 190.
14 Hutchison op cit. p.183.
15 War Diary 2nd Argyll & Sutherland Highlanders PRO WO95/2426.
16 War Diary 1st Middlesex Regiment PRO WO95/2426.
17 War Diary 4th King's Liverpool Regiment PRO WO95/2427.
18 Falls op cit. p.518-519.
19 War Diary D Bn HB MGC 23.4.17 PRO WO95/110.

Chapter 9

ROEUX
APRIL-MAY 1917

The Battle

Roeux was a small village, astride the Arras-Douai railway line. The river Scarpe meandered past it to the west and to the south, and in the east the ground was dominated by a ridge the British called Greenland Hill. In the village was a small chateau and an agricultural chemical works. This had two tall brick towers, north and south of the railway line, and beneath the village was a system of tunnels which the Germans had greatly enlarged. It was to prove one of the most formidable parts of the Arras battlefield in April and May 1917.

In the opening phase of the attack the 4th Division had taken Fampoux and reached a position just east of the village. The sunken lane to the north had also been taken, along with the Hyderabad Redoubt. Between here and Roeux was largely open ground: an attack was planned for 11th April to move forward, take Roeux, Pelves and Greenland Hill. A six hour bombardment was placed on the ground around the Chemical Works and the chateau in Roeux and it was decided to attack in daylight, as few of the troops knew the ground. Meanwhile, the troops from 10th Brigade assembled in the area of the sunken lane, but were soon spotted by German aeroplanes which brought in heavy shell-fire. However,

... the attack... was pressed with extraordinary gallantry and determination by the two first-line battalions, the 1/R Irish Fusiliers and 2/Seaforth Highlanders, which went forward regardless of withering fire from the chateau, the Chemical Works, the station and the embankment. One party of the Fusiliers got to within two hundred

Roeux village, 1916.

189

yards of the station, and the better part of a company of the
Seaforths, led by Lieutenant D.Mackintosh, reached a trench just
west of the first objective, the Roeux-Gavrelle road. Isolated and
having run out of ammunition and bombs, both attempted to
withdraw, but for the most part were shot down... the total
casualties in the Brigade were over one thousand, those of
Seaforth Highlanders being 12 officers and 363 others ranks out
of 12 officers and 420 other ranks who went into action. A long
line of Highlanders could be seen lying where the machine guns
had caught them.[1]

Donald Mackintosh was born in Glasgow in 1896, the son of a local
doctor. He was at Fettes College when war broke out and initially
joined the Royal Army Medical Corps, rising to the rank of Sergeant.
Commissioned into the Seaforth Highlanders in 1915, he served at
Ypres before he was wounded in March 1916. After recovering he was
posted to the 2nd Battalion on the Somme and stayed with them until
the action at Roeux. His body was not found until the village was
finally taken in May 1917. The citation for his VC reads:

On 11 April 1917 north of Fampoux, France, during the initial
advance, Lieutenant Mackintosh was shot through the right leg,
but although crippled, continued to lead his men, and captured
the trench. He then collected men of another company who had
lost their leader and drove back a counter-attack, when he was
again wounded and although unable to stand, nevertheless
continued to control the situation. With only 15 men left he
ordered them to be ready to advance to the final objective and
with great difficulty got out of the trench, encouraging them to
advance. He was wounded yet again and fell. The gallantry and
devotion to duty of this officer was beyond all praise.[2]

The 4th Division was relieved by the 9th (Scottish) Division who made
the next attempt on Roeux. Major-General Lukin, commanding the
Division, had wanted more time for a reconnaissance, but was told by
XVII Corps commander that an attack on the position must be pressed
home at 5pm on 12th April. Lukin's plan therefore was to advance on
the area between the railway station and the ruins of an inn in the
village – the first objective – and then send the second waves through
to take the Chemical Works, Mount Pleasant Wood to the south-west
and the main body of the village itself. But there were bad omens from
the start,

... though the troops had not been engaged since the 9th April,
they had suffered severely from cold, wet, exposure and lack of

hot food, especially in the South African Brigade. Many of the men in this brigade had to be listed to their feet and rubbed by their comrades that morning before they could stand.[3]

In an observation post, observing for his Royal Field Artillery brigade, R.B. Talbot-Kelly, saw the

... attack by the Highland Brigade on the Roeux Chemical Works. The attack started in bright sunshine; the noise of the supporting barrage being largely drowned by the strong gusty west wind which muffled the sound to everyone upwind. Almost immediately the assaulting infantry ran into German machine-gun fire from guns shooting at very long range across the Scarpe from the south. From where I was sitting... the noise of the German machine-guns was completely inaudible and, as I watched, the ranks of the Highlanders were thinned out and torn apart by an inaudible death that seemed to strike them from nowhere. It was peculiarly horrible to watch; the bright day, the little scudding clouds and these frightened men dying in clumps in a noiseless battle. The attack failed completely.[4]

The South Africans had fared even worse. In assembling in Fampoux village in what the Divisional history called an 'evil position', they were swept with shell-fire. Indeed,

... the action that followed was calamitous. The firing of the heavy guns during the day never rose to the intensity of a bombardment, and the large collection of buildings around the

Fampoux, 1917.

191

Station remained quite intact, only one shell being seen to fall near the Chemical Works. There was absolutely no chance of success from the outset, and the uncomplaining heroism of the men was on that account the finest feature of the battle.[5]

With heavy casualties in all the assaulting battalions, the Division was withdrawn from the line. The Chemical Works had proven elusive again.

Major General Harper's 51st (Highland) Division had been out of the line on rest since the start of the battle and it was they who relieved the 9th Division opposite Roeux. The positions they took over were less than desirable, many being in full view of the enemy during the daylight hours and under regular bombardment. Harper was given orders that his men would attack from these positions, and advance on Roeux – finally capturing the Chemical Works and the village. His 153rd Brigade would attack on the left, opposite the Chemical Works itself, with 154th Brigade on the right. They would attack Mount Pleasant Wood and enter the village to the south.

Zero Hour was at 4.45am on 23rd April 1917, when the 'the most savage infantry battle' the 51st (Highland) Division fought in began. Initially, operations on the left went well, and 7th Gordons Highlanders took the initial defences and took many prisoners. However, the 7th Black Watch on their flank ran into heavy machine-gun fire and were unable to push on. Meanwhile, in the area of 154th Brigade, the situation was obscure. It was thought some men had got into the wood and even into the village, but it was confirmed that 4th Seaforth Highlanders had got into the Chemical Works with the help of a tank. This tank, armed with two six-pounder guns, was commanded by a sergeant and greatly assisted the infantry who were fighting their way through the rubble. The Chemical Works now in the hands of the Highlanders, they pushed on to establish a line east of the village, and at one point elements even reached the final objective close to Greenland Hill.

However, as the reserves began to move up to occupy what was thought to be an already consolidated position, they came under heavy fire and it was soon apparent that the Germans were back in the Chemical Works. The foothold made earlier in the day had been heavily bombarded and counter-attacked, and at one point Germans had emerged from tunnels below Roeux into and amongst the Highlanders; an entire section of 152nd Coy MGC was cut off, surrounded and taken prisoner. It was a very confusing situation and, as the day progressed, battalion sized counter-attacks were coming down the slopes of Greenland Hill towards the village. Most were brought down by shell and machine-gun fire from the Highlanders positions. During the night another attempt by 4th Seaforths was made to clear the Chemical Works, but this failed and, as the Division was relieved by the 34th Division, the positions held were in a small area around the railway and a trench line east of the Gavrelle-Roeux road. This fighting had cost the Division an estimated 2,000 casualties.

With the 34th Division in the line, it was decided to continue with the fighting for Roeux and the Chemical Works. However, this was a different Division to that which had fought on the first day of the battle some weeks previously; its ranks now were made up of reinforcements just arrived from the base who had not seen action before. There was also not much time to prepare for the attack and little time to lay down a sufficient bombardment. Set for 4.25am on 28th April 1917, it was later recorded that the Divisional commander, Major General Nicholson, noted

> ... the day is classed as a thoroughly bad one... It began badly, continued badly, and ended worse. The only bright spot was the defeat of a counter-attack on the 101st front... the whole attack line was met by such terrific machine-gun fire that it was doomed to failure from the start.[6]

A few men made it into the German trenches and the 11th Suffolks got to the houses near the Chemical Works, but in most cases there was little success. At one point a German counter-attack threw the men out of the village and they were seen retiring in the direction of Mount

Strongpoint in the Roeux Chemical works 1917.

Pleasant Wood, closely followed by six lines of German infantry. Lance Corporal H.A.L Riggall, of the 10th Lincolns (Grimsby Chums) brought his Lewis gun into action and held on until his gun was knocked out and all his crew became casualties. He managed to escape and was awarded the Military Medal for his bravery. The counter-attack was eventually held by the 10th Lincolns and the nearby 20th Northumberland Fusiliers. With attack and counter-attack, the fighting continued until the 34th Division was relieved on 1st May. By that time they had suffered more than 2,600 casualties.

Roeux and the Chemical Works finally fell on 11th May, right at the end of the battle. The assault was carried out by the 4th Division, who had been in action almost continuously since the start of Arras. Their losses had been so great that the divisional commander could only muster 2,444 officers and men to make the attack, which left no room for a battle reserve. It was do or die.

> The survivors of the infantry battalions were physically so exhausted that some of the battalion commanders were inclined to question their ability to carry out another operation. The prospects of the new plan appealed to them so strongly, however, that their spirits rose, and bodily fatigue was forgotten.[7]

This time the bombardment was heavier and better directed. Artillery was on loan from several formations and there were numerous siege guns from the Corps artillery. Indeed,

> ... when the hour came they went forward close behind the huge wall of fire, the thickest barrage any of them had ever seen.[8]

As a consequence the attacking battalions achieved all their objectives with minimal loss. In one part the Germans held out until the next day, but Roeux and the Chemical Works had finally been taken. With the village won, the 1st Hampshires found something which explained why so many of the previous attacks had failed in the grounds of the chateau.

> Some two hours after the capture of the chateau, men of the 1/Hampshires noticed movement at its south-east corner, and were just in time to stop a party of Germans mounting a machine-gun in a concrete structure with walls six feet, and roof seven feet, in thickness. It had three embrasures for machine-guns to fire in all directions with very extensive command; for, concealed as it was amid ruins, it had been built much higher than the casemates in the Hindenburg Line. Inside were four guns. This 'pill-box' type was already known in Flanders, and was to become all too familiar there.[9]

The Germans, however, were not giving up Roeux without a fight. Units of the 51st (Highland) Division returned to Roeux, with elements from the 17th (Northern) Division. A strong German counter-attack with a fresh division retook the Chemical Works, but was itself thrown back by the northern battalions, with 10th West Yorks re-occupying the ground around the Chemical Works and inflicting heavy losses on the Germans with their Lewis guns as the enemy withdrew. It was a bloody conclusion to a bloody battle. In a month's worth of fighting, five divisions had fought here, two of them twice and nearly 8,000 men had been killed or wounded. It had truly become one of the greatest killing fields of the Arras battlefield.

A Walk on the Roeux Battlefield

Part of this walk overlaps with an area visited in Chapter 3; in fact they work very well if completed consecutively and can even be joined up to make one long walk over the course of an entire day. This walk takes less than three hours and starts and finishes in the sunken road north of Fampoux. Cemeteries mentioned in **bold** are listed below.

Park your vehicle outside the Sunken Road Cemetery, which is signposted from the main D42 in Fampoux village. Walk to the back of the cemetery where the Cross of Sacrifice is located. From here you have excellent views towards Roeux and Greenland Hill and the ground over which 2nd Seaforths and 1st Royal Irish Fusiliers advanced on 11th April 1917. Return to

1. Sunken Road Cemetery
2. Seaforths Memorial
3. Brown's Copse Cemetery
4. Crump Trench Cemetery
5. Roeux British Cemetery
6. Site of Chemical Works

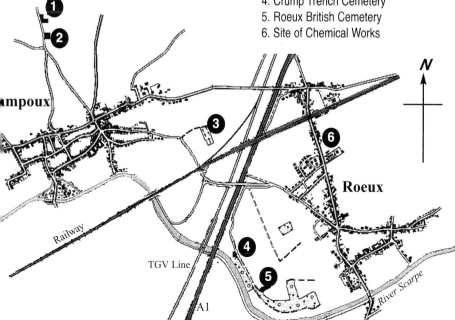

the road and turn left, going downhill. Stop at the Seaforths Memorial, which commemorates the men from the regiment who fell around Arras during the Great War. As the road comes into Fampoux, go straight across at the main cross-roads, and follow this road round to the left until it takes you out of the village. Past Fampoux, the road bends to the right; take a track across the fields to **Brown's Copse Cemetery**.

Return to the road, and turn left, and follow the road under the railway bridge, and then take the bridge which will take you across the TGV line and motorway. This part of the battlefield has changed dramatically in recent years, but just past the bridge is a sanctuary away from the noise of the cars and trains! Take the next minor road on your right, and follow back towards and then alongside the motorway until it becomes a track and follows an embankment into a wooded area. First you will see **Crump Trench Cemetery**, and then continue along the track until it reaches **Roeux British Cemetery**.

Retrace your steps back to the main road and follow it into Roeux village. There is a massive system of tunnels beneath the village and at one time access to them could be gained via a local café. However, this closed some time ago and the last surviving member of the family that owned it died during the preparation of this book. It is hoped that something will be done with these tunnels in the future so that they may be seen by a wider audience.

At the cross-roads in front of the church go left and take the D33 through the village. Further on, you will see a minor road on your left. Take this road to the large German bunker, which once formed part of the Roeux defences. It once sat isolated in open ground, where the incredible field of fire from it could be appreciated. Recent building has obscured the view and the bunker is now sealed up. Return to the D33 and continue to just before the railway crossing. On your right is a French supermarket, with some tennis courts behind. This was once the site of the Roeux Chemical works. When the author first visited the Arras battlefields in the early 1980s the remains of the Chemical works were still visible – a pile of grass covered rubble, over which sheep normally grazed. Helmets and old bayonets could be found amongst the undergrowth, along with a large number of live shells. Sadly sometime in the early 1990s the site was sold and the current development built. Perhaps it is progress?

Cross the railway and turn left at the next crossroads. Here follow the D42 back into Fampoux and at the next cross-roads, turn right and return to the sunken road and your vehicle.

German bunker, once part of the Roeux defences, photographed in 1982. It is now dwarfed by a modern housing estate.

Close up of the bunker in 1982, showing shell damage. Within was an entrance to the Roeux tunnel system. It is now sealed up.

Remains of the Chemical Works in 1982; in the 1990s the site was cleared and is now a supermarket and tennis courts.

Brown's Copse Cemetery, Roeux.

BROWN'S COPSE CEMETERY, ROEUX

Brown's Copse Cemetery is half a mile west of the village of Roeux, between the railway station and Fampoux. It is named from a nearby small copse, the Bois Rossignol. Plots I to IV are made up almost entirely of isolated graves cleared from the Arras battlefield in the summer of 1917. Plots V to VIII were made after the war by the concentration of some 850 graves from an area around Arras. Burials now total: 1,923 British soldiers, 129 South Africans, two Canadians and one whose unit was not identified. There are 856 unknown graves and nine Special Memorials.

The following were concentrated into Brown's Copse Cemetery:

SEAFORTH CEMETERY, ROEUX: located on the north-east side of the road from the village to the station, eighteen British soldiers were buried here in April 1917 and also twenty-one from the 6th Seaforth Highlanders who died in August and September 1918.

VITRY-EN-ARTOIS COMMUNAL CEMETERY and GERMAN EXTENSION: a cemetery in which seventeen British soldiers, largely officers of the Royal Flying Corps, were buried by the enemy.

CRUMP TRENCH BRITISH CEMETERY

Named after a nearby trench of the same name, this is a small battlefield cemetery with 182 British burials which was used by front line units in the Roeux area between April and August 1917. By the end of the war, it was found that nearly half the graves had been obliterated by shell fire. Because of this a quarter of the graves here are unknown soldiers and there are thirty-three Special Memorials.

Amongst the burials are several men from the Household Battalion, which was serving with the 4th Division at this time. Second Lieutenant N. Bonham-Carter (II-C-7) was from a well known English family, and was killed with the regiment on 3rd May 1917.

ROEUX BRITISH CEMETERY

This battlefield cemetery was made amongst the shattered trees which bordered on the Scarpe valley in late April 1917. It reflects well the units which fought for the Roeux Chemical works in April-May 1917, and includes one of the greatest number of men from the Household

Battalion buried in one cemetery. Burials total 349 British soldiers, with eighty-two Special Memorials. The latter reflect the fact that this ground was fought over again in 1918 and many graves were damaged by shell-fire. Like its neighbour, Crump Trench Cemetery, it is one of the most peaceful cemeteries on the Arras battlefield.

1 Falls, C. Military Operations France and Belgium 1917 Volume 1 (HMSO 1940) p.270.
2 London Gazette 8th June 1917, PRO ZJ1.
3 Falls op cit. p.283.
4 Talbot Kelly, R.B. A Subaltern's Odyssey: Memoirs of the Great War 1915-1917 (William Kimber 1980) p.158.
5 Ewing, J. The History of the Ninth (Scottish) Division 1914-1919 (John Murray 1921) p.203-204.
6 Shakespear, J. The Thirty Fourth Division 1915-1919 (1921) p.114-115.
7 Falls op cit. p.511.
8 ibid. p.511-512.
9 ibid. p.512.

Barge on the Scarpe river, 1917.

Chapter 10

BULLECOURT
APRIL-MAY 1917

The Battle

As the fighting at Bullecourt has been described in some detail in two recent books on the battle, the description of the engagements here will be much briefer than in previous chapters. Readers are therefore directed to these two books, which are in the bibliography. However, no story of Arras is complete without Bullecourt, and a walk or visit to this area is very much encouraged.

The village of Bullecourt was located in one of the most strongly defended sections of the Hindenburg Line on the Arras battlefield. There were deep trenches here, with thick belts of wire and many concrete structures at ground level, with concrete lined dugouts beneath. The trenches had been well positioned to maximise the fields of fire of the defenders, and the major disadvantage the British had here was that they were largely holding an 'outpost line', north of the Croisilles-Bullecourt-Queant railway line – with open ground beyond and no cover. The Germans commanded the ground, and with it the battlefield.

The Bullecourt battlefield.

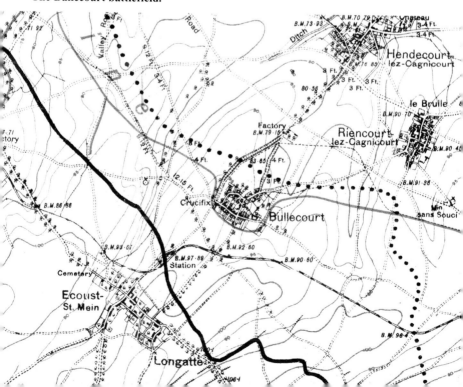

Mine crater on the battlefield near Bullecourt.

For the battle in April – May 1917 it was on the extreme right (or southern) flank, and came under General Sir Hubert Gough's Fifth Army, rather than Allenby's Third Army. Two formations would dominate the fighting here; the 62nd (West Riding) Division of the British Army, and the Australian divisions then under Gough's command as part of I ANZAC Corps. No attack had been planned in this area on the first day of the battle, 9th April, but it had became clear some time before that an advance into the Hindenburg Line at this point would assist Allenby's men further north.

Such an advance was ready for 10th April. On this day the 185th Brigade of 62nd Division, made up of battalions of the West Yorkshire Regiment, made an attack on the strong Hindenburg Line positions immediately in front of the village of Bullecourt with elements of 4th Australian Division attacking on their right flank. In many respects this 'attack' was a large patrol of several West Yorks battalions advancing from the outpost line into the German defences, where they would hopefully meet up with the Australians. Parts of the belt of barbed wire were penetrated, but German machine-gun caused havoc and heavy losses, particularly in the withdrawal which was made once it was realised there was no chance of getting into the German trenches.

Meanwhile, the Australians had fared little better. Previously patrols from the 14th Battalion Australian Imperial Force (AIF), led by the famous Captain Albert Jacka VC MC, the first Australian to get the Victoria Cross in the Great War, had reported the Hindenburg Line intact and well-manned by the enemy. It was therefore planned to lay down a heavy bombardment on the ground to be attacked and the Australians would also have the benefit of tank support from the Heavy Branch Machine Gun Corps. The troops allocated for the assault were put in assembly positions and trenches beyond the front line where they were to wait for the tanks to arrive. The tanks got delayed on the way up and the weather turned worse from thick snow to snow blizzard at one point. It was hardly ideal conditions to be lying out in and as the tanks were so late it was decided to abandon the operation. However, in making their way back to the front line, the Australians were seen emerging from the assembly positions and came under a heavy fire. Thankfully there were few casualties; the battle would be renewed the next day.

The 11th April dawned cold, with snow still in evidence. Nearly a dozen tanks were detailed to assist the advance of the 14th, 16th, 46th and 48th Battalions AIF in their advance on the Hindenburg Line.

A tank from D Company Heavy Branch Machine Gun Corps knocked out at Bullecourt on 11th April 1917.

Another view of the same tank.

Most were late in arriving, and unable to assume the attack position in front of the infantry. What followed was a disaster. The majority of these tanks either broke down, were disabled or knocked out. C.E.W. Bean, the Australian official historian, noted:

> ... *so far as it was known... all the tanks – with the exception of that which entered Bullecourt – had fought their short fight in the area rear of the Australian front line... their carcasses could be seen motionless, and in most cases burning, all over the battlefield.*[1]

Meanwhile the infantry had attempted to make the best of the situation, despite the failure of the tanks. The 16th Battalion AIF had been led into battle by Major Percy Black DCM. A veteran of Gallipoli, and often referred to as the 'bravest man in the AIF', he had said to his men,

> ...*'come on boys, bugger the tanks!'... under a hurricane fusillade, he led his men through the wire.*[2]

Black and his men captured the German front line and just as he was about to begin the advance on the next line of trenches he was shot in the head and killed.[3] On their right the 46th Battalion had also breached the Hindenburg Line and Lieutenant Colonel Ray Leane's 48th Battalion then passed through them on to the second line. This was taken and held for a short distance, but it soon became apparent that the Australian position was precarious. Short of ammunition and bombs their footholds in the German line soon came under counter-attack and it was soon clear a withdrawal was necessary. The biggest problem with this was the evacuation of the wounded; many of which had to be left behind this. Among them was Captain Leane, brother of the commander of 48th Battalion. He died some time later in a German hospital; Leane's other brother had been killed in the debacle on 10th April; Bullecourt had proved a costly experience for the Leane family. 'First Bullecourt' had been a costly experience for the Australians generally. In one action they had lost more than 3,000 men, more than one third of them taken prisoner – the greatest number in any single action for Australian troops during the entire period of the war.

The Second Battle of Bullecourt broke at 3.45am on 3rd May. Major General N.M. Smyth's 2nd (Australian) Division would attack on the right directly towards the Hindenburg Line between Bullecourt and Riencourt. On the left was Major General Braithwaite's 62nd (West Riding) Division who would assault the trenches on the western and north-western side of the village.

One feature of the Australian attack was the large deployment of Vickers machine-guns, with units borrowed from 5th (Australian) Division to lay down a huge machine-gun barrage. It was also well supported with artillery. Despite this, on the right front of 5th Australian Brigade, the attack failed with heavy losses. Bunching had occurred in the darkness and, whilst the wire was cut, cross machine-

British dead from the 62nd (West Riding) Division in the German trenches.

Sunken lane full of Australian troops near Bullecourt.

gun fire had turned the battlefield into a killing zone. Confusion caused panic as C.E.W. Bean later noted,

> ... somewhere near the centre some officer lost his head – many men reported that they had been met by him with the order 'Pull out – retire – get back for your lives.' ... The word to 'pull out' ran along the front. The rear waves had no notion of what had happened ahead of them, but seeing the front running back on them... they too ran back.[4]

While attempts to rally the troops were made these failed and the attack broke down.

On 6th (Australian) Brigade's front the wire was also well cut and the men effected an entry into the main Hindenburg Line. However, heavy fire threw the 22nd Battalion back. But Brigadier General J. Gellibrand, commanding the brigade from the railway embankment overlooking the battlefield, was able to commit reinforcements and

wisely realised that, despite the reports coming in, the 5th Brigade on his right were not where they should have been. Meanwhile Gellibrand's men continued the advance, but were again met by withering fire. The open flank on their right caused problems and units did not advance much beyond a cross-road of tracks below Riencourt. The general failure prompted the Divisional commander to send in more men from 7 Brigade, but Gellibrand realised the situation was useless and persuaded the battalion commander of this unit only to send a small group forward. When they were wiped out no more men were sent. In the positions already gained the ebb and flow of battle carried the men backwards and forwards all day, with attack, counter-attack,

View of the Bullecourt battlefield in mid-1918.

and attack once more. By the conclusion of the day the survivors '…
exhausted by the long struggle… awaited the relief which they so well
deserved'.[5]

Meanwhile on the front of 62nd (West Riding) Division all three
brigades attacked simultaneously, supported by tanks from D
Company Heavy Branch Machine Gun Corps. The right attacking
brigade succeeded in entering Bullecourt village, but smoke caused
loss of direction and heavy machine-gun fire on the 186th Brigade
positions in the middle forced this unit to retire. Some troops made it
to their objectives beyond Bullecourt, but with both flanks in the air
most were surrounded, cut off and killed or taken prisoner. The tanks
had proved of limited help; one had entered the village but was hit and
set on fire and others, although reaching the German lines, had found
no supporting infantry and, due to the failure of the attack, had
therefore withdrawn. By the conclusion of the day's fighting the
Division was back in its trenches and had suffered over 3,000
casualties.

Bullecourt had been a failure except for the capture of positions in
the Hindenburg Line by 6th (Australian) Brigade. Nearly 15,000
Australian and British troops had become casualties here since the
beginning of the battle and this forgotten right flank of the Arras

Officers of the 2nd Queen's on the Bullecourt battlefield, May 1917.

battlefield had become a moon-scape of shell holes and smashed ground, well described by a British unit which relieved the Australians in May 1917:

> By this time Bullecourt and its surroundings had become a veritable charnel house; dead bodies and dead mules lying around in hundreds, and the place so offensive that it was a question whether it could be retained.[6]

A Walk on the Bullecourt Battlefield

This walk takes about four hours (excluding time spent in the Bullecourt museum) and visits the main areas fought over by the Australians and British troops from 62nd (West Riding) Division. Several cemeteries are visited, but there are a number outside of the area of the walk which should be seen in follow-up visits with a car. Cemeteries in **bold** are mentioned below.

Park your vehicle close to **Croisilles British Cemetery**. There are parking bays in the road that leads to the cemetery close to a local football pitch. Having visited the cemetery rejoin the road and go right, walking uphill. Soon on the left is a footpath that follows the route of the old Croisilles-Bullecourt railway line. Take this track and follow it across the next minor road to where it runs along an embankment. Below to the right you will see **Croisilles Railway Cemetery**; access to this cemetery via steps is planned, but may not yet be in place. Otherwise continue to where the track meets the main road (D5); go straight across and continue. Where it meets the next track turn right and follow this to the main road (D5), and turn right – **Ecoust St Mein British Cemetery** is on your right.

Leaving the cemetery retrace your steps to the old railway line and follow it along the next section of the embankment. The 7th Division occupied this reserve position when it came into the line here after the main fighting for Bullecourt. Follow the track to the next road and then turn right and take a path, doubling back on yourself, to visit **Ecoust Military Cemetery**. Return to the road (D5E) and follow it out of the village. Past the grain silos stop and look ahead and to the left; you are looking at the ground fought over by 62nd Division on 3rd May 1917.

Continue into Bullecourt and turn right into rue d'Arras. Follow this almost to the end; the last house on the left is No 1 rue d'Arras. M. Jean Letaille lives here, and his private museum of the Hindenburg Line fighting and the Battle for Bullecourt is open most days. It does not have strict opening hours, but it is just a matter of introducing yourself and asking M. Letaille to open the museum. He is a very nice

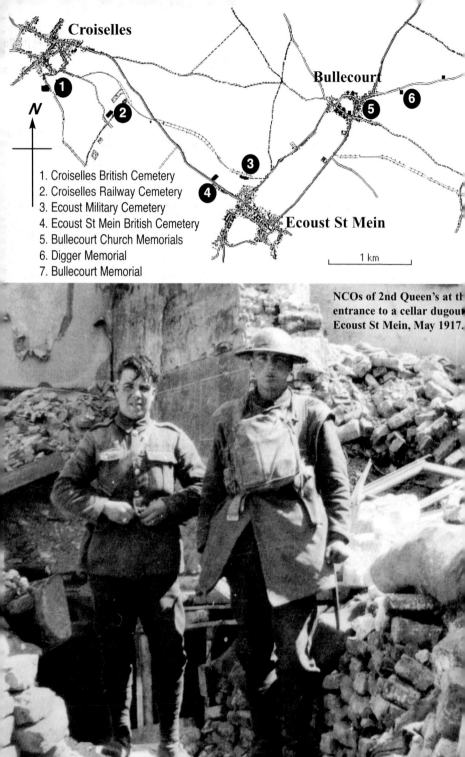

Croiselles

Bullecourt

6

5

N

1. Croiselles British Cemetery
2. Croiselles Railway Cemetery
3. Ecoust Military Cemetery
4. Ecoust St Mein British Cemetery
5. Bullecourt Church Memorials
6. Digger Memorial
7. Bullecourt Memorial

Ecoust St Mein

1 km

NCOs of 2nd Queen's at th
entrance to a cellar dugou
Ecoust St Mein, May 1917.

and kind individual and former mayor of the village. His knowledge of the ground and the battle here is second to none and he and his late wife were awarded the Order of Australia for their services to returning Australians over many, many years. M. Letaille's incredible collection has everything in it from bits of the Hindenburg Line bunkers, to sections of tanks and tank tracks from some of those knocked out at Bullecourt on 11th April 1917. Entrance to the museum is free, but donations are welcome.

Leaving the museum turn left and go to the cross-roads. Go straight across and follow the track out of the village. Where the houses end, stop. Here you have a good view across the ground fought over by Australian troops on 11th April and 3rd May – and the ground where eleven tanks were knocked out. Continue for some distance to a cross-roads of tracks and here turn left. This track roughly parallels the direction of the advance on 3rd May. At the next junction turn left onto a minor road and follow this

CQMS of 2nd Queen's at his dugout on the railway embankment at Ecoust, May 1917.

back towards Bullecourt. En-route you will see the unofficial Memorial to the Missing of Bullecourt; this was an idea of André Coilliott, owner of a fine private museum in Arras, and John Laffin, one of Australia's most prolific historians. Historian and author Tony Spagnoly was also involved. Built in 1982 it is now covered with plaques commemorating those who fought here in 1917. Later you will see the more recent 'Digger' memorial which was built between 1992/93. It takes the form of a huge bronze figure of an Australian soldier, designed by Peter Corlett, and based on his own father who fought in the battle. Every year the village holds a service of

The railway embankment at Ecoust, May 1917.

Officers of the 2nd Queen's on the railway embankment, Ecoust, May 1917.

remembrance here on ANZAC Day. It was to the rear of this memorial site that the remains of Sergeant Jack White were found (see below).

Stay on this minor road. Where it joins the D956 go left and continue to the church. In front is the 'Slouch Hat' memorial which was made in the 1980s to commemorate all the British and Commonwealth units which fought at Bullecourt during the First World War. Go to the main cross-roads in the village and retake rue d'Arras to the right. Follow this to the edge of the village and then at the next cross-roads go straight across in the direction of Croisilles. Follow this to the high ground, stop and look back. Again you have good views across the British sector of the battlefield.

Continue to the D5 and turn right and then take the first turning on the left. Follow this to the end and then re-take the old railway line track following this back to **Croisilles British Cemetery** and your

A veteran returns: an old soldier of the RGA revisits Bullecourt in the 1920s.

Memorial to the missing soldiers of Bullecourt.

vehicle.

CROISILLES BRITISH CEMETERY

The 7th Division attacked Croiselles in March 1917, and took it on the 2nd April in a snow blizzard. The village was lost on 21st March 1918 and retaken by the 56th (London) Division, after heavy fighting, on 28th August. The British Cemetery is on the South side of the village, close to the railway line. Plots I and II were made between April 1917 and March 1918; the rest of the cemetery was formed after the war by the concentration of eighty-six graves from the neighbouring battlefields and from some smaller burial grounds in the area. The cemetery now contains the graves of 1,147 British soldiers, airmen and sailors of the RND, three Canadian, two South African and one Australian; with sixteen German soldiers and two men of the Chinese Labour Corps. There are sixty-four unnamed British graves, and fourteen Special Memorials to British soldiers buried among them. Other Special Memorials record the names of several British soldiers once buried in Hendecourt-les-Cagnicourt communal cemetery in 1917 whose graves were destroyed by shell fire. The burials in the cemetery are dominated by the Guards, 7th and 21st Divisions.

Plot I, Row A, is dominated by four officers and twenty-two men from 2nd Queens who died in the capture of Croiselles on 2nd April 1917. The 16th (Irish) Division served in the area in November 1917 and among their dead is Lance Corporal C.G. Shier (II-B-15), 7th Royal Irish Regiment, who died on 30th November 1917, aged twenty-nine. The inscription on his grave reads, 'killed while helping a wounded comrade under heavy shell-fire'.

CROISILLES RAILWAY CEMETERY

The railway which runs from Croisilles to Bullecourt forms a high and long embankment before it reaches the Croisilles – Ecoust road. To the south of this embankment a military cemetery was started by units of the 7th Division in April 1917. It remained in use until January 1918 and when the ground fell into German hands in March 1918, they buried twenty-five soldiers here, with the final burial being made by British troops in September 1918. Graves total 180 British, and twenty-six German. There are twenty-seven unknowns, and one Special Memorial.

The very first burials are from 21st Manchesters (Manchester Pals) in Plot I, Row A. The 16th (Irish) Division made a small diversionary

attack near Bullecourt in November 1917, as part of the Battle of Cambrai, and burials from this formation are particularly noticeable here. The last burial was Lieutenant R. Donaldson MC (II-B-1) of Anson Battalion in the Royal Naval Division. He was killed at Inchy on 5th September 1918, aged twenty-five, and had been an Arts and Science student at Glasgow University before the war.

ECOUST MILITARY CEMETERY

Ecoust St. Mein was captured by the 8th and 9th Devons on 2nd April 1917, and lost to the Germans on 21st March 1918 when the ground was defended by the 59th Division. It was retaken by the 56th (London) Division at the end of the following August. The Military Cemetery is on the north side of the village, immediately south of the railway embankment. It was started by units of the 7th Division in April 1917 and used by fighting units until March 1918. The Germans then used it to bury their dead and after the war seventy-five British graves, almost all of the 2/6th North Staffords who fell on 21st March 1918, were added to Plot II, Row B, from a position just outside the cemetery. It now contains the graves of 140 British soldiers, nine from Australia and seventy-one Germans. There are seventy-two unnamed graves and one Special Memorial.

The 62nd (West Riding) Division is well represented in this cemetery with casualties from

The Digger Memorial, Bullecourt.

the fighting at Bullecourt on 10th/11th April and 3rd May 1917. Later casualties include Lieutenant Colonel T.B.H. Thorne (II-B-20) who died commanding 2/6th North Staffs on 21st March 1918, aged forty-four.

ECOUST ST MEIN BRITISH CEMETERY
Ecoust British Cemetery was originally made in the continuation of a German Extension (now removed) of the Communal Cemetery. It contains the graves of 145 British soldiers (largely 2nd Suffolks and 13th King's Liverpools of the 3rd Division) and six from Canada; seven of these graves are unnamed. Many of the burials here are 'collective' graves, men buried together in 'mass graves' after the fighting near the village in 1918. As such there is often more than one name on each headstone.

HAC CEMETERY, ECOUST ST MEIN
HAC Cemetery was started by units from the 7th Division following the fighting for Ecoust when twenty-seven men from 2nd Battalion Honourable Artillery Company (Infantry) who, with one exception, had died between the 31st March and 1st April 1917, were buried in what is now Plot I, Row A of the cemetery. Following the German counter-attack near Lagnicourt on 15th April, twelve Australian gunners were buried in the same row. Rows B, C and part of D were then made in August and September 1918 when the ground had been

HAC Cemetery, Ecoust St Mein.

recaptured by the 3rd Division; but many burials then were also from the 56th (London) Division. These 120 graves therefore made the original HAC Cemetery. After the war 1,725 graves were added from the surrounding battlefields of Bullecourt and Ecoust and from a number of smaller burial sites. Burials now total 1,508 British soldiers, 162 Australian, twenty-six Canadian, four New Zealand and 145 whose unit was not known. There are 1,086 unknown graves and sixty-five Special memorials; fourteen of them to Australians.

The following cemeteries were among those concentrated into HAC Cemetery:

BARASTRE COMMUNAL CEMETERY GERMAN EXTENSION: contained 284 German graves, forty-six French, and those of thirty-nine British soldiers, four from New Zealand and one from Australia.

BULLECOURT CHURCHYARD: contained the graves of two British airmen.
BULLECOURT GERMAN CEMETERY: south of the village, just beyond the railway line, in which 200 German soldiers and thirty British soldiers were buried.

CAGNICOURT COMMUNAL CEMETERY GERMAN EXTENSION: contained 333 German and six Russian graves, and those of seventeen British soldiers, and one from Australia.

CROISILLES GERMAN CEMETERIES: both were on the road to Ecoust, and contained the graves of some 505 German soldiers, one French, and eleven British soldiers.

EPINOY CHURCHYARD: contained the graves of three British airmen and one Soldier from Canada, as well as 136 German graves. The church was destroyed in the war, and the Churchyard was closed to further burials.

IMPERIAL CEMETERY: about half a mile west of Hendecourt-les-Cagnicourt it contained the graves of ten British soldiers and two men from the RND along with seven Canadian soldiers, all of whom died in August and September 1918.

INCHY-EN-ARTOIS CHURCHYARD: this contained the grave of one Royal Naval Air Service officer.

LECLUSE CHURCHYARD: this contained the grave of one RFC officer.

L'HOMME MORT CEMETERY No 2, ECOUST ST MEIN: located between the position called L'Homme Mort and Vraucourt village, it contained the graves of 19 British soldiers who died in August and September 1918.

MARQUION GERMAN CEMETERY: located in the village of Marquion. It contained the graves of 211 German soldiers, eight Russian, and 17 British soldiers.

MORY-ECOUST ROAD CEMETERIES No 1 AND No 2, ECOUST ST MEIN: both were very near the Mory-Ecoust road. They were used between March and May 1917, and contained the graves of sixty-three British soldiers (almost all from 8th and 9th Devons, and RFA units of the 7th Division) and one from Australia.

QUEANT GERMAN CEMETERY: located at the north-east exit of the village, it contained the graves of twenty-two British soldiers who died in March 1918.

VILLERS-LES-CAGNICOURT COMMUNAL CEMETERY: contained the graves of twenty-five German soldiers and two British.

MORY ABBEY CEMETERY
Mory Abbey Cemetery is opposite a large farm called 'L'Abbaye' (which still shows some traces of the old pre-1914 buildings). The 189 German burials in a Plot on the west side of the cemetery were made by German units between March and August 1918 or, in thirteen cases, by British troops in September 1918. The British Plots were started at the end of March 1917 and carried on by fighting units until March 1918 and then again in August and September. The 287 graves (including many of the Guards Division killed in August 1918) in Plots IV and V were added after the war by the concentration of graves from the battlefields between St. Leger and Bapaume. The grave of one United States airman was removed to another burial ground; possibly the American Somme Cemetery at Bony. Graves now number: 616 British, one from Australia and one from New Zealand. There are 101 unnamed graves, and one Special Memorial.

Lieutenant Elias Tremlett DSO (I-G-4) served with the 9th Devons and 208th Company Machine Gun Corps. He had also fought at

Gallipoli and on the Somme with the 4th Worcesters. Killed by shell-fire near Bullecourt, his family published a small 'in memoriam' booklet about him in the 1920s called 'Trem' – the name by which the family knew him.

Among the 1918 burials is Captain R.A.West VC DSO MC (III-G-4). He had served with the North Irish Horse before transfer to the Tank Corps. His Victoria Cross citation reads:

Captain R.A.West VC DSO MC

For most conspicuous bravery, leadership and self-sacrifice. During an attack, the infantry having lost their bearings in the dense fog, this officer at once collected and re-organised any men he could find and led them to their objective in face of heavy machine-gun fire. Throughout the whole action he displayed the most utter disregard of danger, and the capture of the objective was in a great part due to his initiative and gallantry.[7]

The following cemeteries were among those concentrated into Mory Abbey:

GRENADIER GUARDS CEMETERY, ST. LEGER: on the road to Vraucourt, it contained the graves of twenty-four men of the 2nd Grenadier Guards and two other British soldiers who died on 27th August 1918.

HALLY COPSE EAST CEMETERY, ST. LEGER: located between a position known as Hally Copse and the road to Vraucourt it contained the graves of forty-nine British soldiers (all from the Guards Division except one) who died in August 1918.

MORY FRENCH CEMETERY: nearly half a mile south-west of the village where three British soldiers were buried in February and March 1917.

NOREUIL AUSTRALIAN CEMETERY

Noreuil was the scene of a heavy fighting involving the Australians in April 1917. After the war it was adopted by the British town of Petersfield, Hampshire, but there does not appear to be any connection between them today. The Australian Cemetery is near the southern outskirts of the village, on the east side of the road to Morchies. It was started at the beginning of April 1917 and used until the following December. Four burials were also made in September 1918. It contains the graves of 182 Australian soldiers and sixty-two British, but twenty-eight are unnamed and eighty-two, destroyed by shell fire in 1918, are represented by Special Memorials. These eighty-two graves are almost all from 50th Battalion AIF who fell nearby in April 1917.

Among the Australian burials are two brothers. Angus and Thomas Boston (Special Memorial 8 and Grave F-41) were the sons of Thomas and Hannah Boston of South Australia. They joined up together in the 50th Battalion, served together and died together on 2nd April 1917.

QUÉANT ROAD CEMETERY
This area was reached by the Third Army on 2nd September 1918 following the storming of the Drocourt-Quéant line by the Canadian Corps. Quéant Road Cemetery is on the north-west side of the road closer to Quéant village. It was started when the 2nd and 57th Casualty Clearing Stations operated near here in October and November 1918. It then consisted of seventy-one graves (now Plot I, Rows A and B). The cemetery was greatly enlarged after the war by the concentration of 2,226 graves from the battlefields of 1917-1918 between Arras and Bapaume and from certain smaller burial grounds – particularly close to the battlefield of Bullecourt. Burials now total: 1,248 British soldiers, 954 Australians, eighty-seven Canadians, two British West Indies, one New Zealand grave and five men whose unit is not known. The graves of two soldiers and one airman of the United States forces were removed to another cemetery in the early 1920s. There are 1,443 unnamed graves and forty-three Special Memorials to Australians;

Queant Héninel Road Cemetery.

with thirteen to British soldiers. There are twenty-six other Special Memorials to British soldiers once buried in German cemeteries in the neighbourhood whose graves could not be found on concentration.

In the mid 1990s an additional burial was made here when the body of Sergeant John James ('Jack') White (VIII-B-28A) was discovered on the Bullecourt battlefield close to the Digger Memorial. Identified by an intact 'dog tag', it was discovered that his daughter was still alive in Australia. She came out for the subsequent funeral, which was organised jointly by the CWGC and Australian Army. Jack White artefacts are on display in the museum at Bullecourt.

The following cemeteries were among those concentrated into Quéant Road:

BARALLE COMMUNAL CEMETERY BRITISH EXTENSION: which was made in September 1918 and contained the graves of twenty-five British soldiers. Two graves were also brought in from the GERMAN EXTENSION in the same cemetery.

CAGNICOURT COMMUNAL CEMETERY: it contained the grave of one British soldier who died in September 1918.

LAGNICOURT (6th JAEGER REGIMENT) GERMAN CEMETERY: nearly a mile east of the village it contained 137 German graves and one British.

NOREUIL BRITISH CEMETERIES No 1 and No 2: these were located close together about 400 yards north of Noreuil village. They were made between April and August 1917 and contained the graves of fifty Australian soldiers and sixteen British, but some of these were re-buried in the HAC Cemetery at Ecoust St. Mein (see above).

NOREUIL GERMAN CEMETERY No 1: next to Noreuil Australian Cemetery it contained seventy-eight German graves and ten British.

PRONVILLE GERMAN CEMETERY: located near a position called The Cave, on the western outskirts of Pronville village, it contained seventeen British graves.

PRONVILLE GERMAN CEMETERY No 4: located a mile south of Pronville, on the road to Beaumetz, it contained eighty-three German and eighty-three British graves (fifty-two of the British were from the Black Watch).

PROVILLE CHURCHYARD: contained two British graves.

ST LEGER BRITISH CEMETERY

St Leger was occupied by British troops in the middle of March 1917 and then lost after a stiff defence by the 40th and 34th Divisions during the German Spring Offensive in March 1918. The village was recaptured in August by the 62nd (West Riding) and Guards Divisions. After the war the village of St. Leger was adopted by the Borough of Doncaster; although no connections appear to remain today. St Leger British Cemetery was started in March 1917 and then used by fighting units and Field Ambulances until March 1918 when a certain number of burials were made by the Germans. It contains the graves of 183 British soldiers, one from India and twenty German. Three of the British graves are unnamed and six, destroyed by shell fire, are represented by Special Memorials.

1 Bean, C.E.W. The AIF in France Vol IV (1933) p.316.
2 ibid p.295.
3 The body of Major Percy Black was never found; he is commemorated on the Villers-Bretonneux Memorial.
4 Bean op cit. p.435.
5 Falls, C. Military Operations France and Belgium 1917 Volume 1 (HMSO 1940) p.463.
6 Messenger, C. Terriers In the Trenches: The History of the Post Office Rifles (Piction Publishing 1982).
7 London Gazette 29th October 1918.

APPENDIX 1
ARRAS CEMETERIES

This section of the book examines some of the key Arras cemeteries which fall outside the area of the main chapters but which contain many casualties from these battle areas. It also includes details of the Arras Memorial, where the majority of those who fell in 1917 are commemorated.

ARRAS MEMORIAL
The Arras Memorial is located next to the Faubourg-d'Amiens Cemetery (see below), in the Boulevard du General de Gaulle, west of the main city centre and close to the Citadel, a French army barracks. There is parking, but visitors are advised not to leave valuables, as there have been many break-ins here in recent years.

Arras Memorial to the Missing, Faubour d'Amiens Cemetery.

The Arras Memorial commemorates 34,734 soldiers from Britain, South Africa and New Zealand who fell in the Arras area from the spring of 1916, when British troops first arrived, until 7th August 1918, who have no known grave. The missing from 8th August onwards are on the Vis-en-Artois Memorial. Most of the dead are from the April-May 1917 Battle of Arras, or are those who died in the March 1918 operations. A separate section of the memorial, the Arras Flying Services Memorial, commemorates nearly a thousand airmen of the Royal Naval Air Service, Royal Flying Corps and the Royal Air Force, who were shot down along the whole Western Front (including Belgium), and who have no known grave. The memorial was designed by Sir Edwin Lutyens, with sculpture by Sir William Reid Dick.

There are thirteen Victoria Cross winners commemorated here, among them four who won their awards at Arras. Naval names from the Royal Naval Division's actions at Gavrelle are also found here, along with South Africans who fought at Arras with the 9th (Scottish) Division. Arras has one of the highest proportions of missing for any British sector of the Western Front, with a high percentage of those who fell in the April-May 1917 battle commemorated on this memorial.

ACHICOURT ROAD CEMETERY

Achicourt Road Cemetery is located at the crossroads of the D919 from Arras to Bucquoy and the D5F from Beaurains to Achicourt. It is located down a grass path between houses and some allotments.

Achicourt Road Cemetery was started in March 1917 and remained in use until June; the graves of these four months are in Rows A to C, and forty-three of them, out of sixty-eight, are those of officers and men of the London Regiment from units in the 56th (London) Division. The cemetery was used again in August and September 1918, when Rows D and E (containing fifty-nine graves, of which fifty-one are Canadian) were made. Four more graves, from Achicourt Churchyard Extension, were added to Row E after the war. Burials now total seventy-eight British soldiers, fifty-two from Canada and one whose unit is not known. The only substantial burial ground moved here was:

ACHICOURT CHURCHYARD EXTENSION: it contained the graves of about a hundred French soldiers, and three British plus one from Canada. It was on the north side of the Churchyard.

AGNY MILITARY CEMETERY

Located in the grounds of Agny Chateau, the village of Agny once also contained also some British graves at the "Railway Arch" north of the village (now removed to Douchy-les-Ayette British Cemetery) and a German cemetery of more than a thousand graves (also removed) at Pont-Ficheux, where the Arras-Amiens road crosses the railway line. Agny Military Cemetery was started by the French and used by British units and Field Ambulances from March 1916 to June 1917. Two further burials were made in April 1918; and in 1923-24 some 137 graves were brought in from the surrounding battlefields east of Arras. The forty French graves were removed in the 1920s. Burials total 407 British soldiers, one from Australia and five German prisoners. The 118 unnamed graves are almost all among those that were brought in from the Arras battlefields after the war.

The most visited grave in this cemetery is that of Great War poet Second Lieutenant Philip Edward Thomas (C-43). Edward Thomas, an important poet and writer even before 1914, joined the Artists' Rifles in 1915 and was commissioned into the Royal Garrison Artillery, serving with 244th Siege Battery at Arras. He was killed near Neuville-Vitasse on 9th April 1917, aged thirty-nine, while spotting for the battery. The blast of a shell sucked all the air from his lungs and stopped his heart. There was not a scratch on his body, which was brought back to Agny for burial by his men.

BEAURAINS ROAD CEMETERY

Beaurains is a village on the southern outskirts of Arras, and Beaurains Road Cemetery is just north of the village on the road from Arras (N37). Beaurains was captured, after only slight resistance, on the 18th March 1917 and the cemetery was begun a few days later. The cemetery was used, sometimes under the name of Ronville Forward Cemetery, when the Battle of Arras began up until the beginning of June 1917. The burials were made by fighting units and also by the 14th (Light) Division Burial Officer. It was used again for a short time in August and September 1918, in the Second Battles of Arras. At the end of the war burials totalled: 129 British soldiers, fifteen French soldiers and four German prisoners. The cemetery was then enlarged by the concentration of 188 graves from Ronville British and French Cemeteries, and from the surrounding battlefields. Burials now total: 303 British soldiers, fourteen from Canada and four Germans. There are twenty-three unidentified graves and fourteen Special Memorials to men once buried in Ronville British Cemetery, whose graves were later destroyed by shell fire. The main cemeteries moved here were:

RONVILLE BRITISH CEMETERY: located among the houses in the Faubourg St. Sauveur, a little south of the Bapaume road. It was used between April and July 1917, when most of the burials were made by the 20th King's Royal Rifle Corps, and by the 141st Field Ambulance RAMC in August and September 1918. It contained the graves of 167 British soldiers, twelve from Canada, and nine Germans.

RONVILLE FRENCH CEMETERY: it adjoined the British Cemetery and was used from February to April 1917 and again in August 1918. It contained the graves of twenty-six British soldiers.

DAINVILLE BRITISH CEMETERY
Dainville is village west of Arras, on the road to Doullens (N25). The cemetery is about one kilometre west of the main village and located at the end of a track running north from the road to Warlus (D59). Some distance from the front, Dainville was a billet for British troops during the fighting near here in 1917 and several Advanced Dressing Stations also operated in the village. Burials at Dainville began in the communal cemetery in March 1916, when British troops first came to the Arras front; and it was again used in April 1918 when the German offensives came close to breaking through. The British Cemetery was started by the 56th (London) Divisional Burial Officer in mid-April 1918 and used by units of the division until they were relieved by the Canadians in July 1918. Burials total 131 British and Canadian and four German.

DUISANS BRITISH CEMETERY, ETRUN
Duisans and Etrun are both villages west of Arras, close to the main St Pol road (N39). Both were used for billeting troops, and a number of Casualty Clearing Stations operated here from 1916 onwards. The main one was 8th CCS, which remained open until April 1918. It was later joined by 19th CCS (which remained until March 1918) and 41st CCS (which stayed until July 1917). The first burials were made in March 1917, but the majority relate to the April-May 1917 period and are of men who died of wounds received in the fighting around Arras. Between May and August 1918 it was much closer to the front and was used by fighting units and Field Ambulances. When the fighting moved on, the 23rd, 1st Canadian and 4th Canadian CCSs opened here and remained for two months until October/November 1918. The 7th

CCS then came to Dusians, and stayed until long after the end of the conflict. British and Commonwealth graves now total 3,205, along with eighty-eight Germans who died of wounds whilst prisoners of war.

Any visitor to this cemetery will soon note the battle damage on the main entrance. This was caused when the area was fought over in May 1940. A small field gun was set up in the cemetery, and the entrance took direct hits from German tanks and guns.

FAUBOURG D'ARRAS CEMETERY, ARRAS

The Communal Cemetery in Arras, located in the suburb of St. Sauveur, on the east side of the city, was under fire during the Great War. Civilian burials were made in the French Military Cemetery which was opened near the Citadel in the western suburb called the Faubourg-d'Amiens. This Military Cemetery (named from the Military Hospital in the Convent of the St. Sacrement) contained in the end the

Faubour d'Amiens Cemetery in 1919.

graves of 770 French soldiers. Behind it there grew up, from March 1916 to November 1918, the present British Military Cemetery. It was made by Field Ambulances and fighting units. It was increased, after the war, by the concentration of 111 graves from the battlefields of Arras and from two smaller cemeteries and at the same time the French graves in front of it were removed to other burial grounds. Two of the British graves were destroyed by shell fire and are represented by special memorials. The third special memorial commemorates an officer of the United States Army Air Force who died during the Second World War.

The two cemeteries from which British graves were taken to Faubourg-d'Amiens Cemetery were the following:

LIGNEREUIL MILITARY CEMETERY: located on the outskirts of the village, beside the road to Aubigny, which was begun by French troops and contained the graves of seven soldiers from the United Kingdom.

RUE-ST. MICHEL BRITISH CEMETERY, ARRAS: in the eastern part of the town, containing the graves of eighty-nine soldiers from the United Kingdom and two from Canada who fell in April and May 1917.

Lieutenant-Colonel A.J.Sansom.

Captain Gilbert Nagle MC

This is an important Battle of Arras cemetery, because with a high proportion of known burials it gives us a much better cross-section of the men and units which fought at Arras in 1917. Among the burials are some interesting stories and some tragic ones. Lieutenant Colonel Alfred John Sansom and his Adjutant Captain Gilbert Nagle MC, were standing at the entrance to their headquarters' dugout on Infantry Hill at Monchy-le-Preux when a stray shell burst between them. Sansom was fifty years old and formerly the headmaster of a school in Hastings. He had in his pocket a letter informing him that the War Office was sending him home, after two years on the Western Front, to resume his duties as headmaster. In

Plot I is an unusual grave of a Russian soldier, taken prisoner on the Eastern Front and forced to work on the Hindenburg Line by the Germans. In February 1917 he escaped and approached the British lines near Arras, then being held by the 7th Royal Sussex. Seeing him and another in No Man's Land, the Sussex soldiers called out a challenge. The answer in Russian they mistook for German, and opened fire. This man was killed and his friend wounded!

MAROEUIL BRITISH CEMETERY
Maroeuil is located north-west of Arras, between the roads to Houdain and Aubigny. The British Cemetery lies at the end of a track running north from the road to Bray and Ecoivres (C1). The village was used to billet troops out of the line around Arras and Heavy artillery units were also based here. The cemetery was started by units of the 51st (Highland) Division when the British army took over the Arras front in March 1916, and it retained its association with that Division until the summer of 1918. Nearly one half of the graves are those of Highland Territorials. Nearly one quarter are those of London Territorials, from 60th (London) Division, who were here from July to December 1916 while they occupied the front near Vimy Ridge. Men from Tunnelling Companies of the Royal Engineers are also well represented with twenty-five officers and men buried here; and the 6th Seaforths, the 6th Argyll and Sutherland Highlanders and the 5th and 7th Gordons once erected memorials to officers and men of their own units who perished in mine explosions. These are no longer here. The cemetery was protected from observation by the crest of the hill behind it; and whenever it was possible bodies were brought back to it from the front line by tramway. The Cemetery contains the graves of 531 British soldiers, thirty from Canada, one from India, one Chinese labourer; and eleven Germans.

ST NICHOLAS & STE CATHERINE BRITISH CEMETERIES
Sainte Catherine and Saint Nicolas are villages adjoining the city of Arras to the north side, Ste. Catherine lying to the west and St. Nicolas to the east of the main road to La Targette and Souchez. From March 1916 they were in British occupation and during the greater part of that time they were within the range of German artillery fire. The Cemeteries were made and used by the British Divisions and Field Ambulances stationed on that side of Arras. Ste. Catherine British Cemetery is in open country on the left of the Roman road to Therouanne (the Chaussee Brunehaut), not far beyond the church. It

was started in March 1916 and contains the graves of 312 British soldiers, thirty-two Canadians, two South Africans, one Australian, one of an unknown unit and one German prisoner. Rows A to E, two graves in Row F and five in Row H are the original cemetery, disused in the autumn of 1917. The remaining 203 graves were concentrated into the cemetery after the war, some from the country immediately north-east and east of Arras, some from south-east of St. Laurent-Blangy and a large group from a point on the left of the Therouanne road, a little south of La Targette.

St. Nicolas British Cemetery is on the rue d'Enfer, which joins the road to Roclincourt. It was started a year later, in March 1917, and was used until October 1918. It contains the graves of 350 British soldiers, nine South Africans, three Canadians and two Australians. Eighty of these belonged, or were attached, to Artillery units, reflecting the use of the ground that surrounds the cemetery. Two memorial crosses were once erected here; one to an officer and thirteen men of the 9th Seaforth Highlanders (Pioneers), killed in action on the 6th June 1917, and one to three officers and fourteen men of the 2nd Essex Regiment, who fell in a raid on the enemy lines on the 9th August 1917. Both have been removed and their fate is unknown.

Germans launch a counter-barrage with a 21cm howitzer.

230

Right: Officers of the Royal Berkshire Regiment outside the ruins of the town hall at Arras.

The fighting at Arras has not produced the same level of literature as the Somme or Ypres. However, in recent years there has been a resurgence of interest in the area and there have been several books on specific areas in the 'Battleground Europe' series; among them *Bullecourt, Gavrelle, Monchy-le-Preux, Vimy Ridge and The Battle for Vimy Ridge*. Other useful books include:

Anon., *Arras* (Michelin Tyre Company 1919)
The first guide to the area, published shortly after the war. Reprinted in the late 1990s and easily available.

Duclos, J-L. L. *Saint Laurant-Blangy dans la Grande Guerre* (Cercle Archéologique Arrageois 2001)
A title in the French series covering the fighting around Arras which looks at St Laurant Blangy, one of the key front line locations on the edge of the city. Profusely illustrated, with numerous maps and plans. Text in French. Available from the Tourist Office in the Hotel de Ville in Arras.

Gliddon, G. *VCs of the First World War: Arras & Messines 1917* (Alan Sutton 1998)
Part of an excellent series, the book examines all the Arras Victoria Cross winners and gives details of their background and the action which resulted in their award.

Jacques, A. (Ed) *La Bataille D'Arras: Avril-Mai 1917* (Cercle Archéologique Arrageois 1997)
The first in an excellent series of French books on the battle. Text in French, with the exception of an article by Christopher Pugsley on the New Zealand Tunnellers. Profusely illustrated.

Nichols, J. *Cheerful Sacrifice: the Battle of Arras 1917* (Leo Cooper 1990) Sadly this is the only book on the battle and despite a lack of detailed historical analysis, it is worthwhile for the superb veterans' accounts.

Girardet, J-M, Jacques, A & Letho Duclos, J-L. *Sur l'axe stratégique Arras-Cambrai: Tilloy-les-Mofflaines, Monchy-le-Preux* (Cercle Archéologique Arrageois 1999)
Partner volume to Alain Jacques' earlier work, this is also in French. However, it is an excellent study of the area, with some good illustrations. Available from the Tourist Office in the Hotel de Ville in Arras.

Girardet, J-M, Jacques, A & Letho Duclos, J-L. *Somewhere On The Western Front: Arras 1914-1918* (Cercle Archéologique Arrageois 2003) A new English edition which combines some of the material in the earlier books by the same authors, along with newer information, including articles on some of the archaeological work around Arras in recent years. Also available from the Tourist Office in the Hotel de Ville in Arras.

Walker, J. *The Blood Tub* (Spellmount 1998)

An excellent modern account of the fighting for Bullecourt and not just from the Australian perspective.

Light railway running along the banks of the Scarpe river at Arras. Royal Engineers bridging a section of the Scarpe river, April 1917.

Wounded at a dressing station at Blangy.

The ruins of Arras.

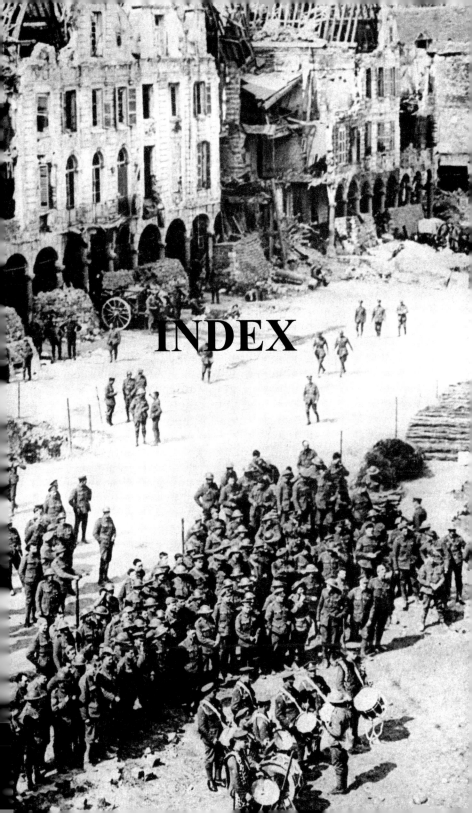

INDEX

Previous page: A band from 12th (Eastern) Division plays to passing troops in Barbed Wire Square, Arras April 1917.

236